# Math & Stories

# Math & Stories

**Marian R. Bartch, Ph.D.**

**Illustrated by Street Level Studio**

*An Imprint of ScottForesman*
*A Division of* HarperCollins*Publishers*

## Dedication

for Aaron and Catherine Weddle

GoodYearBooks
are available for most basic curriculum subjects plus many enrichment areas. For more GoodYearBooks, contact your local bookseller or educational dealer. For a complete catalog with information about other GoodYearBooks, please write:

GoodYearBooks
ScottForesman
1900 East Lake Avenue
Glenview, IL 60025

Book design by Street Level Studio.

Printed in the United States of America.

ISBN 0-673-36317-1

1 2 3 4 5 6 7 8 9 - MH - 03 02 01 00 99 98 97 96 95

# Table of Contents

# About Math & Stories

The purpose of this book is to assist teachers in integrating children's literature, mathematics, and language. It is designed to connect the teaching of mathematics to other curricular areas in a natural and logical way. The benefit to students is two-fold—they learn to appreciate the finest books in the literature available to them and they then understand that mathematics is not an isolated subject, but is related in many ways to their other studies and to their daily lives. Thus the development and understanding of mathematical skills and concepts is extended and strengthened.

The mathematical activities in the book encompass twelve of the thirteen standards developed and recommended for implementation for grades K–4 by the National Council of Teachers of Mathematics. These standards are:

- **Mathematics as Problem Solving**
- **Mathematics as Communication**
- **Mathematics as Reasoning**
- **Problem Solving as Making Connections**
- **Estimation**
- **Number Sense and Numeration**
- **Concepts of Whole Number Operations**
- **Whole Numbers Computation**
- **Geometry and Spatial Sense**
- **Measurement**
- **Statistics and Probability**
- **Patterns and Relationships**

Each story unit lists the standards and concepts covered in the mathematical activities stemming from the sharing of the book. Language activities that emphasize the skills of reading, writing, listening, and speaking are also included for each title. In addition, there are pre-reading and post-reading discussion questions for the teacher's use. The activities and exercises also encompass the seven kinds of multiple intelligences, which are:

- **Logical–mathematical**
- **Linguistic**
- **Spatial**
- **Bodily–kinesthetic**
- **Musical**
- **Intrapersonal**
- **Interpersonal**

Activities may be organized in a variety of ways appropriate for different learning and grouping preferences and purposes—individual work, cooperative learning groups, working with partners or in small groups, and whole-class activities. Many of the activities for the lower primary levels are teacher-directed and are most effective when used with whole-class participation.

Books and activities need not be limited to a single grade level. However, the units are arranged in order from those most appropriate for Kindergarten children to those most appropriate for third grade. Allowance is made for a cross-cutting and overlapping of these levels as the interests and abilities of students vary widely within a single classroom. It is those abilities and interests at the various levels that will determine which of the activities are best for which children.

## Structure of Each Unit

**1) Title**

**2) Standards and Concepts**

**3) Story Synopsis**

**4) Materials List**

**5) Introduction**

**6) Mathematics Activity**

**7) Follow–Up Activities**
- **Mathematics**
- **Language**

### Title
The books chosen are notable for the quality of text and illustrations as well as containing a high level of interest to young students. They are almost exclusively either Caldecott or Newbery award or honor books so that they should be readily found in school libraries.

### Standards and Concepts
The mathematical standards and concepts that relate to the book and are the focus of the activities are listed next.

### Materials
All materials needed to implement the activities are listed after the story synopsis. You can make some substitutions if a different, or more readily available, type of material is more appropriate to use with a particular class or group. Activities are on reproducible sheets for convenience in copying, making transparencies, and distributing. Note that all metric conversions are approximate.

### Story Synopsis
The story line of each book is given in a complete and detailed format. This is not intended as a substitute for reading the book, but to enable you to decide, when pressed for time, if a specific book is appropriate for your class.

### Introduction
The pre–reading discussion questions are designed to generate interest in the book about to be shared; post–reading discussion questions are designed to focus on some of the important aspects of the books and/or to stimulate interest in the forthcoming activities. Additional titles for extended reading and class organization for various activities are also included.

### Mathematics Activity
The mathematics activity that relates most directly to the story is described first. However, you may change the sequence of the activities as you wish. The mathematics activities emphasize a specific application of the hands–on approach to generate an understanding of a mathematical concept and also to focus on the various areas of the multiple intelligences.

### Follow-Up Activities
A second, or alternate, mathematics activity is also provided, and again, is to be used at your discretion. A language activity, related to the book, is also provided. Specific language concepts are not listed but are designed to strengthen and extend communication skills through journal writing, creative dramatics, listening skills, and, of course, reading.

### Answer Key
This book includes an answer key to allow students to check their work. However, a great number of the activities are open–ended and require no check, for answers will be varied. They are included to permit students to develop their own creativity, to stretch their imaginations, and to assist them in feeling confident in their ability to work with and see meaning in mathematics.

AUTHOR:
**Lois Ehlert**

STANDARD:
**Geometry and Communication**

CONCEPT:
**Identify Common Shapes in the Environment, Manipulate, Color, Fold, and Create Simple Geometric Shapes**



## Materials:

- Construction paper in a variety of colors, several for each student
- Paper plates, crayons or markers, glue
- Scissors
- Popsicle® sticks—one for each student
- "Shape Animals" activity sheet
- "Where Should These Animals Be?" activity sheet
- Transparency of the "Where Should These Animals Be?" activity sheet
- "My Imaginary Animal" activity sheet
- Contact® paper, shoe boxes, and black construction paper for each student (optional)
- Attribute and/or pattern block pieces for each student

# COLOR ZOO

**The author/illustrator has devised a cut-out format to create a series of zoo animals who take form as the pages are turned. For example, a triangle, square, and circle are overlaid so that a tiger is transformed successively into a mouse, and the mouse transformed into a fox in three pages by the removal of one cut-out shape at a time. The front of each page reveals the name of the animal while the back reveals the name of the shape and the cutout of the shape itself. The fourth page is for the child's use in creating an original animal and shows the three shapes and their names. There are nine different animals—tiger, mouse, fox, ox, monkey, deer, lion, goat, and snake. The ten shapes are the star, circle, square, triangle, rectangle, heart, oval, diamond, octagon, and hexagon. Sixteen different shades of color are also shown on one of the last pages. The design of this very original book should stimulate the imagination and creative nature of each student.**

## Introduction

Initiate a discussion of the various shapes the class has been studying—perhaps having individuals identify some simple shapes found in the classroom. The following may be used as a basis for discussion before sharing the book with the class:

1. Ask children to think of an animal they know and tell if that animal's face is like one of the shapes you have been studying or one you see in the room.
2. Ask: Do you think you could start with a certain shape and make an animal face from it? Would this be hard to do? Why or why not?

Introduce the book to the class by explaining that the author/illustrator has combined shapes and colors in an almost magical way to create the animals they will see. Then share it with them. After the class has viewed and enjoyed the book, ask the following questions:

1. How many shapes can you name that were in this book?
2. Do you have a favorite shape? What is it? Why?
3. Did the book show any of your favorite animals? Which?
4. Are these animals ones you have seen at the zoo?
5. Are these animals like any you have ever seen anywhere before? Where?

## Mathematics Activity

Provide each student with three full-sized sheets of construction paper in various colors and attribute or pattern block pieces of various shapes to use in the creation of a "Shape Animal," along with scissors, crayons or markers, and glue. Shapes may be made by combining the different colored papers and gluing them together to imitate the book, or in any other way the student may wish.

Tell students before they begin work on the activity page, "Shape Animals," that they may draw a picture of their animal and glue it on a second piece of paper, or trace around a pattern they may have made from blocks, and to write or print the name of their animal under its picture.

The design of the animals may follow those in Ehlert's book or any other kind of design. Animals may be purely imaginary. Give students the option of including the names of the created animals in the design.

Books can be made from the construction-paper pictures to be displayed, then taken home. If books are to be made students should be shown how to fold the sheets in half (following along as the process is demonstrated to them) before creating their animals and to position the paper with the fold to the left. Papers folded in that fashion can then be stapled along the left edge.

Display the finished products on a bulletin board entitled "Our Classroom Zoo" or made into individual books to be displayed, then taken home. A "Zoo Train" may also be created using shoe boxes turned on their sides and covered with Contact® paper or decorated with crayon or markers. Cut and glue strips of black construction paper, or "cage bars," to the top and bottom of the open side and place the animal in the box.



## Follow-Up Activities

The activity sheet "Where Should These Animals Be?" involves students in identifying a shape, and recognizing its name, used in *Animal Zoo* to create a specific animal face. A review of the book immediately prior to assigning this activity will provide a necessary reinforcement for some students. Use a transparency of the activity sheet, which allows students to follow along as you explain. There are two columns, one with the name of an animal, the other with the shape used. Students listen as you read the names in both columns to them. Reread each animal name to them one at a time. They are to find the names of the shapes of the animals listed in Column One in Column Two and copy those names in the blanks in Column One. When students have filled in all the names, they should copy the marked letters in the blanks at the bottom of the page. The question will be answered, "In Our Classroom." Explain that not all of the blank spaces will be used when they copy the names of the shapes.

The "My Imaginary Animal" activity is a combined mathematics and language activity. Mathematics is involved in that students will be making size comparisons between the animal and themselves, deciding on the quantity of food their animal will eat, how much the meal costs, and how big a bed the animal would need, using nonstandard measures. (For example, twice or half as big as mine, or six shoes long.) Students will use their written and oral communication skills as well as mathematics skills in completing this activity.

The "My Imaginary Animal" sheet may be duplicated and distributed to the students or they may use a separate sheet of paper, but it will work better as a teacher-directed activity. Allow sufficient time for students to write after you read each sentence in the story. The guidelines may be shortened or modified to fit the abilities and interests of the class.

Students should share their stories about the "shape animal" they have made, adding any information they would like others to know. They may also demonstrate how it moves, how it sounds, and what it can do.

A "Zoo Parade" may be held with each student moving as his/her animal would and taking turns making the kind of noise each would make. A nice addition to the parade is for each student to carry a paper plate mask showing the face of the animal. Eye holes need to be traced, then cut out by an adult before students draw on the features using crayons or markers. A Popsicle® stick glued on the underside makes a nice sturdy holder. Music such as Saint Saens' "Carnival of the Animals" sets the pace of the parade.

Name

Date

ACTIVITY

# Shape Animals

Directions: Use this page for your "Shape Animal."

______________________ Name

______________________ Date

# WHERE SHOULD THESE ANIMALS BE?

Directions: Copy the names of the shapes in Column Two to match the names of the animals in the blanks in Column One. Listen carefully as they are read to you. Not all of the spaces in the blanks will be filled each time. When you finish, copy the letters in each word that appear in parentheses in the blanks at the bottom of the page. If you match them all correctly, you will see the answer to the question, "Where Should These Animals Be?"

| Column One | Column Two |
|---|---|
| 1. Tiger _ (_) _ _ _ _ _ _ _ _ | CIRCLE |
| 2. Fox _ _ _ _ (_) _ _ _ _ _ | DIAMOND |
| 3. Snake _ _ _ _ _ _ (_) _ _ _ | HEART |
| 4. Mouse _ _ (_) _ _ _ _ _ _ _ | HEXAGON |
| 5. Ox (_) _ _ _ _ _ _ _ _ _ _ | OCTAGON |
| 6. Deer _ _ _ (_) _ _ _ _ _ _ | OVAL |
| 7. Goat _ _ _ _ _ _ (_) _ _ _ | RECTANGLE |
| 8. Monkey (_) _ _ _ _ _ _ _ _ _ _ | SQUARE |
| 9. Lion _ _ _ (_) _ _ _ _ _ _ | TRIANGLE |

Where should these animals be? _ _   _ _ _ _   _ _ _ _ _! YES!!

Here is a picture of the animal I like best in the book. It is the ______________________.

Name ______________________ Date ______________________

ACTIVITY

# MY IMAGINARY ANIMAL

Directions: Now that you have created your great (and maybe scary) imaginary animal, you need to think about what this animal will need to stay with you in your house.

Give it a name that it will like.

My animal's name is ______________________________________.

I am calling it that because it ______________________________________.

It makes a noise that sounds like ______________________________________.

It will eat __________ dishes of ______________________________ each day.

My animal is not the same size that I am. I am __________ tall and weigh __________ pounds/kilograms.

It is ____________________ tall and weighs ____________________ pounds/kilograms.

Its bed must be ____________ long and ____________ wide, and will be a __________ color.

We will have fun together doing ______________________________ and

playing the game of ______________________________________.

This is a picture of my animal.

AUTHOR:
**Pamela Allen**

STANDARD:
**Estimation–Measurement**

CONCEPT:
**Weight and Balances**

## Materials:

- Plastic glasses—one per group of four students
- Paper towels and spill–over trays—foil trays or plastic tubs work well
- Small plastic bottles with caps, a cork, coins, crayons in a plastic bag—a supply for each group
- Plastic bags of jelly beans, crayons, and M&M's® for each group
- Balance scale for each group
- "Keep Your Head Above Water" activity sheet
- "Tipping the Scale" activity sheet
- "We Sank the Boat!" activity sheet

# WHO SANK THE BOAT?

The title of this story suggests that a disaster may be about to happen as Cow, Donkey, Pig, Sheep, and Mouse decide it would be nice to go out on the bay in the rowboat one day. The boat looks very small in comparison to the size of the passengers, but all of them seem willing to try to fit inside it. Cow leaps into the boat first, almost capsizing it then and there. She clings desperately to the edge of the dock and manages to steady herself and the boat. Donkey, being more cautious, is able to achieve just the right balance by backing into the boat and sitting opposite Cow. Overweight Pig upsets that balance and loses her umbrella in boarding. The boat sinks alarmingly low in the water. Sheep, anxious to embark and get on with her knitting, knows exactly where to sit to restore the balance. Mouse's small size and weight surely will not cause the boat to sink—but, oh no! When he steps aboard, the boat goes down immediately! Everyone is dumped into the water and their outing is ruined. The disgruntled would-be travelers trudge home in sad shape. Cow, Donkey, and Pig are dripping wet, and Sheep's ball of yarn is soggy and bedraggled. Mouse, however, has a rather happy look on his face. Surely he didn't plan to ruin the whole outing, or did he?

## Introduction

Before sharing the story, ask students if they can guess what happens by looking at the picture on the cover and hearing the title. Write the predictions on the chalkboard or on overhead transparency film to discuss after the story has been enjoyed.

1. Can you tell what is going to happen in this story? How?
2. How many of the animals should try to get into the boat? Is there any special order for them to step into it that would keep it from sinking? What?
3. Will the boat sink? When?
4. What will happen to the animals if the boat sinks?

When you're finished with the book, check to see how accurate the predictions were.

## Mathematics Activity

Plastic glasses or other containers that will hold water and spill–over trays are needed for the "Keep Your Head Above Water" activity. Organize students in small groups, with each group having one plastic glass filled with water to within one inch (2.5 cm) of the top.

**Trial 1:** Students make an estimation of which of the materials provided will sink and which will float. Then they conduct trials to confirm or not confirm the estimates. They make comparisons between the number estimated and the actual number used by circling the (yes) or (no) choice. (Only two crayons will be in a bag for this part.)

**Trial 2:** Students repeat the trial with directions to pour some water in the plastic bottles to see if they sink or float. They make estimates first, then repeat the same process of circling after the experiment.

**Trial 3:** The third experiment allows students to see if an increase in the number of crayons in the bag will make the water in the glass overflow. Again, they estimate first, then compare results.

## Follow-Up Activities

The "Tipping the Scale" activity sheet involves the use of a balance—a commercial one or one made from two paper cups suspended from a coat hanger by string. Students will estimate how many jelly beans will be needed to balance the crayons and how many M&M's® balance the jelly beans. They will then record those numbers. They will test each estimate by putting the materials on a balance and checking whether or not they balanced. They will work with the materials until they achieve a balance. They conclude with their ideas on how to solve the problem of what to do with the remaining jelly beans and M&M's®.

LANGUAGE

This is an excellent story to use for creative dramatics. Students form groups of five or six. Allow them time to devise action and, especially, dialogue using the "We Sank the Boat!" activity sheet. Each character in the story must make at least one comment to each of the other characters. Action may parallel that in the book, or may begin with the actual boarding of the boat. Record students' comments on the guide sheet only to focus attention on sequence and to help students think of what they will say. An alternative dramatization may be done as a pantomime as you narrate the action.

**Note:** Use a video camera, if available, to film each group's presentation. Students will enjoy seeing themselves in their performances.

Name

Date

# KEEP YOUR HEAD ABOVE WATER

Directions: Listen carefully, for this activity will be done step by step. First, estimate which of the materials you have will float and which will sink by circling a "yes" if they will float, a "no" if they won't. Test your estimate by putting the materials in the water and then circle a "yes" if they floated, a "no" if they didn't. Repeat this process by estimating, testing, and circling your answers to see if pouring some water in the bottle makes a difference. Again, estimate, test, and circle your answers to see if increasing the number of crayons in the plastic bag will make the water in the glass overflow. Be sure to keep the glass in the tray.

**Fill in the blanks with numbers.**

1. Use each of the materials and estimate which will float and which will sink by circling "yes" if they will float, "no" if they will not.

   **Estimate:** bottle (yes) (no) cork (yes) (no) crayons (yes) (no) coins (yes) (no)

   **Actual try:** bottle (yes) (no) cork (yes) (no) crayons (yes) (no) coins (yes) (no)

   **Estimate was correct:** (yes) (no)

2. Pour some water in the bottle and put on the cap.

   **Estimate:** Wll bottle float? (yes) (no)

   **Actual try:** Did bottle float? (yes) (no)

   **Estimation was correct:** (yes) (no)

3. Add more crayons to the bag, then close it tightly.

   **Estimate:** Will crayons float? (yes) (no)

   **Actual try:** Did crayons float? (yes) (no)

   **Estimation was correct:** (yes) (no)

Our estimates were **(close) (not close)** to the actual results. (Circle one)

The estimates were closer the **first, second, third** time. (Circle one)

We think this is because ______________________________

______________________________________________

Name ______________________ Date ______________________

ACTIVITY

# Tipping The Scale

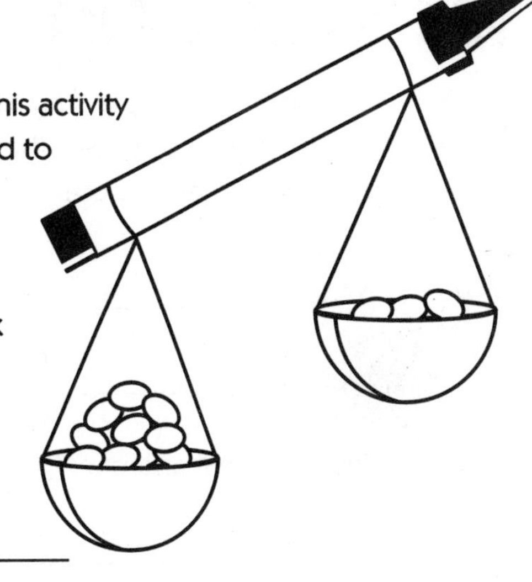

Directions: Listen carefully as the directions are read to you. In this activity you will estimate what amounts of different materials are needed to balance each other. Fill in the blanks with your numbers. Test your estimates by placing that number of objects on the scale. Check the blank that tells if they balanced or did not balance. If the animals in the story had done this, they may not have sunk the boat.

1. Count the number of crayons you put in one cup. __________

   It will take ______________ jelly beans to balance that number of crayons.

   Put the jelly beans in the cup and see if the two cups balance.

   Check here if they did __________. Check here if they did not __________.

   If they did not balance, try again, either adding or taking out jelly beans until they do.

2. Repeat your experiment by filling one cup with jelly beans and try to balance that cup with M&M's®.

   Count the number of jelly beans and write the number here __________.

   It will take __________ M&M's® to balance the jelly beans.

   Put the M&M's® in the other cup and see if the two cups balance.

   Check here if they did __________. Check here if they did not __________.

   If they did not balance, try again, either adding or taking out M&M's® or jelly beans from the cups.

   What do you think you should do with the leftover jelly beans and M&M's®?______________

Name ____________________  Date ____________________

**ACTIVITY**

# WE SANK THE BOAT!

Directions: Each of you who plays an animal in the skit needs to have a general idea of what to say. This guide will help you think about what words you should use.

Cow says to the others ____________________

Others answer ____________________

Cow steps into the boat and cries ____________________

Others call ____________________

Donkey says ____________________

Others answer ____________________

Donkey steps into the boat and yells ____________________

Others answer ____________________

Pig says ____________________

Others answer ____________________

Pig steps into the boat and hollers ____________________

Others answer ____________________

Sheep says ____________________

Others answer ____________________

Sheep steps into the boat and bleats ____________________

Mouse says ____________________

Others answer ____________________

Mouse steps into the boat and they all cry ____________________

AUTHOR:
**Molly Bang**

STANDARD:
**Number and Numeration**

CONCEPT:
**Sequence Counting**



## Materials:

- "Name that Number Now!" activity sheets for the teacher and the students
- "Mother Goose Counts to Ten" activity sheets for the teacher and the students
- A transparency of the "Mother Goose Counts to Ten" activity sheet
- "Lucky for Me" activity sheet
- A set of tagboard numbers 1–10 for each group of students
- Stencils of outlines of numbers 0 to 9 or other patterns to be used in tracing the number outlines

# TEN, NINE, EIGHT

As bedtime approaches, a little girl and one of her parents go through a well-established routine of getting her settled down to sleep. It involves progressing through a very detailed countdown (from 10 to 1) of all of the things associated with bedtime. It begins with **ten** little toes, all clean and ready for bed, then goes on to **nine** favorite friends waiting quietly in the bedroom. Next, **eight** separate panes show in a window which frames the softly falling snow. A big black cat seems interested in **seven** of the girl's shoes that are lined up beside the bed, but the next illustration shows that the cat is really attracted to the six seashells in the mobile hanging over the bed. **Five** different-colored buttons decorate the cheerful yellow sleeper the girl is wearing. There is an indication that someone is getting sleepy as **four** describes eyes slowly opening and closing in a very relaxed way. The girl delights in receiving **three** kisses as she is carried to bed. She puts **two** arms around a favored stuffed animal that she wants to take to bed with her. The last page shows **one** big girl all tucked and snug in her bed. The author has very accurately depicted the often long and complicated process of overcoming the resistance of a youngster who will *never* admit to being sleepy.

## Introduction

Read this book to a small group or show it on an overhead projector in a fiber–optics room if one is available. Emphasize the continuity of the illustrations. Ask students to answer the following discussion questions before reading by a show of hands or by standing up. How many of you:

1. Are never sleepy when it is time to go to bed at night?
2. Always have to go to bed at the same time? Have to be told when it is time to go to bed?
3. Always fall asleep right away?
4. Have a pet, stuffed animal, or toy that you are allowed to take to bed with you? Can sleep better if it is in bed with you?
5. Have someone who stays with you until you go to sleep?
6. Have a favorite bedtime story? What is it?

After sharing the book with the class, ask the following to focus on the numbers 1 through 10. Say the number you have of:

| | | | | | | |
|---|---|---|---|---|---|---|
| arms | knees | lips | mouths | noses | toes | ears |
| heads | elbows | eyes | feet | fingers | hands | |

Then introduce the activity sheet entitled "Name That Number Now!" in the mathematical activity.

## Mathematics Activity

Organize the class in cooperative learning groups of five for using the "Name That Number Now!" activity sheet. Explain to the students that they are going to listen carefully to hear clues in the definitions read to them that will help them decide on the correct number to write in the blank. As you read each definition, students must decide as a group upon the correct number to write. They will take turns (in a clockwise sequence) writing the number. Each student should use a different-colored marker for writing. Provide activity sheets to individuals or have the group share them. When every group is finished, follow with a discussion to allow group members to describe their thoughts as they made their choices.

## Follow-Up Activities

The activity entitled "Mother Goose Counts to Ten" reinforces the concept of the numbers 1 to 10 by focusing on the sound of the numbers as they are used to complete the rhymes. The class may be organized as an entire class, in small groups, or individuals as the activity is worked through. A transparency of the activity sheet helps students follow along as you read the verses. Instruct students to write only the numeral, only the number name, or both in the blanks as they listen to the verses. This may also be done as an oral activity with students saying the numbers as you read the verses.

Ask the class if they remember or know any Mother Goose rhymes. Those who do should recite any that they can. Then the focus could be on the idea that Mother Goose is very interested in numbers.

### One, Two, Buckle My Shoe

One, two, Buckle my shoe;
Three, four, Knock at the door;
Five, six, Pick up sticks;
Seven, eight, Lay them straight;
Nine, ten, A good fat hen;
Eleven, twelve, Dig and delve;
Thirteen, fourteen,
Maids a'courting;
Fifteen, sixteen,
Maids in the kitchen;
Seventeen, eighteen,
Maids a'waiting;
Nineteen, twenty,
My plate's empty.

### One, Two, Three

One, two, three, four, five
Once I caught a fish alive.
Six, seven, eight, nine, ten,
But I let it go again.
Why did you let it go?
Because it bit my finger so.
Which finger did it bite?
The little one on the right.

Once these have been shared and commented upon, introduce the activity sheet by having the class think of at least one word that rhymes with a number from 1 to 10. For example, one–fun, two–do, and so forth. Then instruct them to listen carefully to what they will be hearing. This can be an individual or group activity. The underlined number should be repeated for clarification.

LANGUAGE

A discussion will generate ideas and associations the students have with certain numbers that they believe are important to them. Use the outlines of stencils or tagboard numbers as models on which to base a drawing of their favorite or "lucky" number on the "Lucky for Me" activity sheet. They should fill the blank space inside the outline of the number with words or drawings that tell or show why the number is special to them.

Questions such as the ones that follow will be effective in helping the students to extend their thoughts about numbers:

1. Is there a certain number that you like more than any of the others? What is it?
2. What does this number mean to you? Is it your birthday? The number of people in your family? What?
3. Some people believe that there are certain "lucky" numbers and use them to try to select a winning lottery number. Is there such a thing as a "lucky" number? How do you know?

Tell students that they are to trace or draw in outline the form of the number they have chosen. They then fill the outline with words or drawings that explain this significance. It would be helpful for them to see one or two examples. Instead of an explanation in writing or drawing, students may share their preferences orally.

An alternate activity is to have them work in groups to create their own number rhymes such as writing about the numbers 1 through 10 in story form consisting of one or more lines. Use a pattern such as the following:

Numbers 1 and 10 opened up the number pen. AND THEN 2 and 3 went on a spree; 4 and 5 saw a beehive; 6 and 7 looked around for 11; 8 and 9 were doing just fine UNTIL Numbers 1 and 10 penned them up again!

Janet
Name

July 17, 2007
Date

# NAME THAT NUMBER NOW!

Directions: Listen as the sentences are read to you. Then write a number from 1 to 10 in the blank to complete the sentence.

This number:

1. Tells how many pigs the big, bad wolf met. 3
2. Is the largest number on a die. 6
3. Results when you and a friend count the total number of hands and feet you have together. 4
4. Is the number of noses you have. 1
5. Tells how many dwarfs were friends of Snow White. 7
6. Tell how many days there are in two weeks of school. 10
7. Is the sum of how many mouths you have added to the number of bears Goldilocks met. 3
8. Is 1 less than the number of toes you have on both feet. 8
9. Tells how many fingers you have on one hand. 5
10. Tells how many wheels there are on a bicycle. 2

Name

Date

# MOTHER GOOSE COUNTS TO TEN

Directions: Listen to the rhymes. Then decide which number, from 1 to 10, sounds best to finish the rhyme. Write that number in the blank.

1. There was an old woman
   Who lived in a **shoe**
   The highest she could count
   Was up to ______.

2. Curly Locks! Curly Locks!
   Wilt thou be **mine**?
   Indeed I will,
   As soon as you're ______.

3. Bessy kept the garden **gate**,
   And Mary kept the pantry;
   But it was hard for both of them
   To write that tricky number ______.

4. A robin and a robin's son
   Once went to town to buy a **bun**,
   They had to share the bun they bought,
   Since they could only pay for ______.

5. Wee Willie Winkle runs through the town,
   Upstairs and downstairs in his nightgown.
   "I'm so sleepy, I'm in an awful **fix**,
   How will I ever be able to get up at ______?"

6. Bobby Shaftoe's gone to sea,
   With silver buckles on his knee;
   When he was offered a cup of **tea**,
   He said, "Yes, please, give me ______."

7. All the king's horses
   And all the king's **men**,
   Had to put their heads together,
   To count from one to ______.

8. The Knave of Hearts
   Brought back the tarts,
   And vowed he'd steal no **more**
   He didn't care; he'd already eaten ______.

9. What age may she be?
   What age may she be?
   Twice ten, twice **eleven**,
   No, she's really only ______.

10. About the bush Willie, about the hive,
    About the bush Willie, I'll meet you **alive**;
    If you'll be there at seven,
    I'll be there at ______.

Name ____________________ Date ____________________

# LUCKY FOR ME

Directions: Decide what number is lucky or special for you and draw it in the space below. Make it as large as you can. Fill in the space inside the number with words or a picture that explains why it is a lucky or special number for you.

AUTHOR:
**Nonny Hogrogian**

STANDARD:
**Problem Solving**

CONCEPT:
**Making Predictions and Sequencing**

## Materials:

- 30-40 pieces of 2" by 3" (5 cm by 7.5 cm) tagboard for cards for the Trading Game
- "Simple Simon's Problem" activity sheet
- "Simple Simon" story
- Trading Game directions
- Cuisenaire® rods for the groups and a set of transparent rods for the overhead projector
- Yarn cut in different lengths, one length for each member of the class
- Audio or video recorder

# ONE FINE DAY

**A very thirsty fox has the good luck to see an old woman set down a pail of milk, then turn her back to him. He immediately begins to lap up the milk and—just as immediately—begins to regret this action as she turns around and sees what he is doing. She is so angry that she cuts off his tail! He knows his friends will laugh at him if they see him without his tail, and he begs her to give it back to him. She refuses at first but then relents, on the condition that he replace the milk. This demand causes him to set off on a repetitious journey in which each of his requests are agreed to only on the condition that he give something in return. He finds a cow who will give him milk only if he will give it some grass. He can get the grass only if he will provide water for the field. He can get the water only if someone gives him a jug to carry it in. He can have the jug only in exchange for a blue bead. The blue bead will be given only in exchange for an egg. The hen will give him an egg only in exchange for grain. He is lucky to meet a sympathetic miller, who gives the grain without asking anything in return, and the fox, who is thoroughly exhausted, then reverses his journey to make all of his trades. The old woman then sews his tail on with a very neat stitch, and the fox runs off to join his friends without fear that they will laugh at him.**

## Introduction

Read the first four pages of dialogue up to the last sentence on each page. Ask the students for their predictions on what they think will happen next.

1. Will the cow give him the milk? Why or why not?

Write the predictions on the chalkboard or on overhead projector film before going on. Read the last sentence along with the next page, excluding that last sentence, and ask for predictions once again.

2. Will the fox find the water? What do you think he should do if he cannot find any?

Read the last sentence on that page and record predictions once again. Check predictions again after reading the first sentence on the page on which the fox meets the miller, and record them on the chalkboard.

3. Will the miller want something in exchange for the grain? What might it be? What will the fox do next?

Finish the story. Then lead a discussion about the predictions.

Discuss with the class how the fox solved his problem.

1. What do you think of how the fox solved his problem?
2. Can you think of anything else he could have done to get his tail back?

   What would you tell him if he asked you for help in solving his problem?
3. The fox finally felt so badly that he began to cry. Is this a good way to solve a problem? Why or why not?
4. What do you do when you have a problem to solve? Does this always work for you?
5. Does it help to talk to someone about your problem? Who?

## Mathematics Activity

Explain to the class that it is their turn to solve a problem for someone else. Introduce the activity sheet "Simple Simon's Problem" to the class and tell students that they are going to have to help this old friend solve a problem. Organizing the class in cooperative groups is best for this activity in which they will work toward a solution. Read the problem stated below (or a similar one) to the students. Tell them that they are to think of ways in which to use Cuisenaire® rods to help Simple Simon buy his pie. Distribute the grids and the Cuisenaire® rods to small groups after they have had time to think of some ways to devise a solution to this problem. Groups can take turns showing at least one way they have thought of by using the transparent rods on the overhead projector. The number values of the rods used in determining the equivalences may be recorded as well. Encourage the class to explain the solution in a pattern similar to that in the story they have just heard.

**Problem:**
Simple Simon has met the same pie man that he met once before. This time the pie–man asks Simple Simon to pay for the pie with Cuisenaire® rods. Simple Simon asks what the pie is worth and the pie–man tells him, "An orange and red rod put together." "Oh, no!" exclaims Simple Simon, "then I can't have my pie!" "Why not?" asks the pie man. "Why, because I don't have any orange or red rods with me. The only colors I have are white, light green, purple, yellow, dark green, black, brown, and blue." "Well, then," says the pie man, " it's really simple, Simple Simon. Why don't you trade some of those for the value of the orange and red rods?" "Oh, if I only knew how," cried Simple Simon, "Isn't there anyone who can help me?" Students begin work with the grids and rods.

## Follow-Up Activities

This activity involves the use of the picture trading cards and is for 3 to 4 players. Pictures or drawings are cut to fit 2" by 3" (5 cm by 7.5 cm) cards, which are then laminated. Two of the same pictures or drawings make a match.

### Trading Game Rules

The student who rolls the lowest number on a die shuffles the cards. The player to his or her right deals in clockwise motion until each player has seven cards. The remainder of the deck is placed facedown in the center of the table. A trade is made and a problem solved when the student has two cards with the same picture on each. This makes a pair. Play goes clockwise. A player draws one card from the deck. If that player needs one more card to make a pair, he/she asks another player for that card.

If that player has it, he/she asks, "What will you give me in return?" If that player is satisfied with the answer, a trade is made and the pair is placed face up in front of the first player. If a trade cannot be made, the first player must discard one card from the hand, placing it facedown at the bottom of the deck. Play then goes to the left. The person with the most pairs at the end of the game is the winner.

A practice hand will be very helpful in clarifying the rules. Point out to the students that what they are doing in the game is what the fox had to do in the story, that is, players who want a card must give the person who has it something that player wants in return.

## Follow-Up Activities Con't.

LANGUAGE

This story is a typical "yarn," so use a ball of yarn when telling a story. Explain to the students that the ball of yarn goes from one student to another as each takes a turn in "unwinding" the story as the yarn ball is unwound. When the story is done, rewind the yarn into a compact ball. The best arrangement is for everyone to sit in a circle. Plan the seating arrangement by considering the communication skills of each student. If some students simply cannot think of any way to carry the story forward, let them "pass."

Tell students that they must help solve a problem by finishing a story you begin. Talk until the ball of yarn is unwound. (A little practice in telling the introduction ensures that your part ends when the yarn does.) Then the student to whom the ball of yarn is passed must go on with the story while unraveling a piece of yarn, talking, again, until the piece ends. The ball of yarn is then passed from one student to the next and each continues the story as the yarn unwinds. You may elect to finish the story or have the last student finish it. The story is begun with a problem such as:

> When I woke up this morning and walked into the kitchen, I really had a surprise! There, sitting right at my kitchen table, holding a spoon in his hand, was a monkey. Well, you all know that I do like monkeys but I did wonder what one was doing sitting at my table, so I just asked him what he was doing there. Of course, he couldn't tell me and I didn't really expect him to be able to talk to me. All he could do was to give me a big grin, and that did make me want to keep him. Then I noticed that he was wearing a collar so I knew he belonged to someone else. What should I do? I wondered. Now this may not seem like a big problem to you, but I just have no idea of what to do next, so I thought for a while, then decided to. . . . At this point the story is handed over to the class.

Name ____________________ Date ____________________

ACTIVITY

# SIMPLE SIMON'S PROBLEM

Directions: Simple Simon needs a lot of help to get his pie from the pie man. What can he do? Show him how different rods can be joined together to equal to the orange rod plus the red rod.

Write the combinations of rods you traded for the orange and red rod.

1. ______________________________
2. ______________________________
3. ______________________________
4. ______________________________
5. ______________________________
6. ______________________________

AUTHOR:
**Vera B. Williams**

STANDARD:
**Numbers and Numeration, Problem Solving**

CONCEPT:
**Less Than, More Than, Longer Than, Shorter Than**

## Materials:

- "More or Less?" activity sheet
- "The Long and Short of It" activity sheet
- "More? No? No? More? Who Knows?" activity sheet
- Cuisenaire® rods for students, Cuisenaire® rods for the overhead, and/or Unifix® cubes
- Graph paper
- Markers
- String

# MORE, MORE, MORE, SAID THE BABY

This book is divided into three sections, each of which describes enjoyable activities and obvious affection shared by three very different, very appealing babies and their families.

It is hard for Little Guy's father to keep up with his son who is such a fast runner. When he does, he scoops up Little Guy, swings him around, and then hugs him tightly and kisses him. Little Guy loves this and demands, "More, more, more."

Little Pumpkin's grandmother has trouble trying to keep up with her granddaughter for the same reason. When she does, she picks up Little Pumpkin, holds her nose to nose, and then swings her around. Little Pumpkin delights in this and also demands "More, more, more."

Little Bird is certainly not active in the way the others are, for she sleeps soundly during the entire episode. She nearly rolls off the sofa, and her mother has to move quickly to catch her. She is then held and rocked before being dressed in her nightclothes and put to bed. She is so sleepy that she can only murmur "Mmmmn. Mmmn, mmmn, mmmn."

## Introduction

Introduce the story by telling the students that the book is written about very young children and that they are to try to remember when they were about that age. After sharing the book, discuss the following questions:

1. Did you like to do any of the things these children did when you were a lot younger?
2. Do any of you have any younger brothers or sisters who like to do the things the children did in this story? Do you do any of these things with them? Which?
3. What are some of the things you do now that you would like to do "more, more, more"?
4. How do you think you could persuade a member of your family to let you do these things as much or as often as you would like?
5. Can you remember any time when you wanted "more, more, more" and found out that "more" was just too much? When?

## Mathematics Activity

Do the following exercises before assigning "More or Less?" These exercises give students practice in the concepts *more than, less than,* and *the same as*. Working with the whole-class or medium-sized groups, ask students to make the following comparisons using one-to-one correspondence:

1. Are there more boys than girls in our room? How can we tell? (Boys may be called to stand in the front of the room, then girls called to stand in front of them and the number can be matched.)
2. Are there more of us in this room with blue eyes than any other color? How can we figure this out?
3. Stand up if you are wearing the color red. Are there more or less people standing than are sitting? How do we find out?
4. Stand up and turn around if you like to eat marshmallows. Let's count the number of people standing up. Now sit down. Stand up if you would rather eat mushrooms than marshmallows. Let's count this number. Is it the same? Do more or less people prefer mushrooms to marshmallows?

When students are clear on the concept, direct them to a comparison activity, "More or Less?", in which they will us Cuisenaire® rods to determine what is one more and one less of certain rods named. Instruct them to make a staircase of the rods, beginning with the white rod and ending with the orange one. Then ask the questions on the sheet, such as "Is the length of the white rod more or less than that of the red rod? How much more or less?" Continue with this oral exercise until everyone seems clear on the comparative sizes of the rods. Use transparent rods designed for the overhead and allow various children to have a turn at showing the comparisons and combinations that can be made.

Students may work in groups, pairs, or individually, but this is a teacher-directed activity.



## Follow-Up Activities

The "The Long and Short of It" activity sheet makes connections between students' own lives and the concepts of *longer than* and *shorter than* in relation to their own bodies. This is a teacher-directed activity and will work best if the students are paired or in small groups to help each other in measuring. Tell students that they may use a variety of nonstandard measuring instruments—string, shoes, books, hands, or whatever they wish—to take their measurements. Standard measuring instuments may also be used.

Ask students to think about times that they might want to call "no. no, no" instead of calling "more, more, more." After some discussion, introduce the activity sheet "More? No? No? More? Who Knows?" and instruct students to move to the right side of the room if they think the correct response to the statement should be "no,no,no," and to the left side of the room if the correct response should be "more, more, more." Remind students to move as quietly as possible. Make tally marks on the right side of each statement to record the number of "no" responses and on the left side of the statement to record the "more" responses for a discussion afterwards.

Name

Date

ACTIVITY

# MORE OR LESS?

Directions: Listen as the sentences are read to you. Then use your rods to compare the colors given in each one. Circle the words in parentheses (more) or (less) as you compare.

1. The white rod is one **(more)** **(less)** than the red rod.
2. The orange rod is one **(more)** **(less)** than the blue rod.
3. The light green rod is one **(more)** **(less)** than the red rod.
4. The black rod is one **(more)** **(less)** than the brown rod.
5. The purple rod is one **(more)** **(less)** than the yellow rod.
6. The dark green rod is one **(more)** **(less)** than the black rod.
7. The light green rod is one **(more)** **(less)** than the purple rod.
8. The yellow rod is one **(more)** **(less)** than the dark green rod.
9. The brown rod is one **(more)** **(less)** than the blue rod.
10. The purple rod is one **(more)** **(less)** than the light green rod.
11. The red rod is one **(more)** **(less)** than the light green rod.
12. The red rod is one **(more)** **(less)** than the white rod.
13. The blue rod is one **(more)** **(less)** than the orange rod.
14. The brown rod is one **(more)** **(less)** than the black rod.
15. The yellow rod is one **(more)** **(less)** than the purple rod.
16. The black rod is one **(more)** **(less)** than the dark green rod.
17. The dark green rod is one **(more)** **(less)** than the yellow rod.
18. The blue rod is one **(more)** **(less)** than the brown rod.

Name ______________________ Date ______________________

ACTIVITY

# THE LONG AND SHORT OF IT MEASUREMENT SHEET

Directions: Listen to each sentence. Circle "yes" if you agree with it or "no" if you don't. Then start over and measure that part of your body. Circle the "1" under "yes" if you were right in your guess, or the "2" under "no" if you were not. Write your measurements in the blanks.

1. Your hands are longer than your shoes. Yes 1 No 2

   Hands ______ Shoe ______

2. Your nose is longer than your longest finger. Yes 1 No 2

   Nose ______ Finger ______

3. Your arm is shorter than your leg. Yes 1 No 2

   Arm ______ Leg ______

4. Your wrist is smaller than your ankle. Yes 1 No 2

   Wrist ______ Ankle ______

5. Your eyes are bigger than your ears. Yes 1 No 2

   Eyes ______ Ears ______

6. Your big toe is longer than your thumb. Yes 1 No 2

   Big toe ______ Thumb ______

7. The distance around your waist is smaller than the distance around your head. Yes 1 No 2

   Waist ______ Head ______

8. The length of your arm is shorter than the width of your shoulders. Yes 1 No 2

   Arm ______ Shoulders ______

9. The distance from the end of your nose to your mouth is longer than the distance form your wrist to the end of your middle finger. Yes 1 No 2

   Nose to mouth ______

   Wrist to finger ______

10. The distance from ear to ear is shorter than the distance from your heel to your longest toe. Yes 1 No 2

    Ear to ear ______

    Heel to toe ______

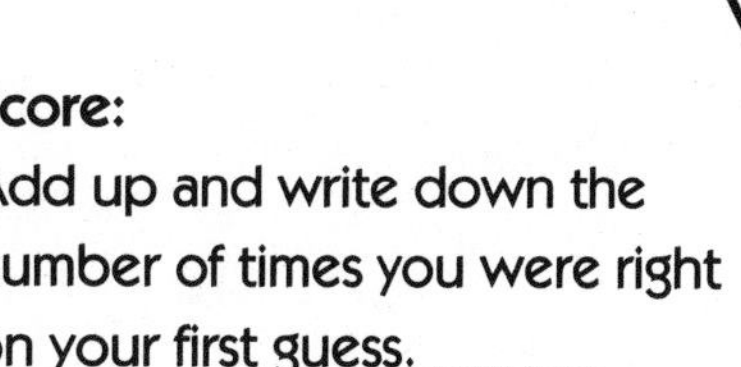

**Score:**
Add up and write down the number of times you were right on your first guess. ______

Name

Date

ACTIVITY

# MORE? NO? NO? MORE? WHO KNOWS?

Directions: Listen to each sentence. If your answer is "no" instead of "more," move quietly to the right side of the room. If your answer is "more" instead of "no," move quietly to the left side of the room. (Make a tally mark at the right side of the statement or question for the number of "no" choices and a tally mark on the left side of it for the number of "more" choices.)

**Would you:**

1. want ice cream?
2. ask for additional helpings of broccoli?
3. like to go to Disney World?
4. like to sleep late?
5. enjoy getting up early on Saturday to clean your room?
6. want to take your little brother or sister to the movies with you and your friends?
7. be happy to give your little brother or sister your favorite stuffed animal?
8. want to have a tooth filled?
9. never want to eat candy again?
10. want to drive a car when you are older?

Number of "Mores" __________

Number of "Nos" __________

AUTHOR:
**Lois Ehlert**

STANDARD:
**Numbers and Number Sense**

CONCEPT:
**Sequence Counting, Addition, Subtraction**

## Materials:

- "Fish Eyes" counters
- "The (Fish) Eyes Have It" activity sheet
- A file folder or a 10" by 16" (25 cm by 38 cm) piece of tagboard to use as the game board
- 20 or more 2" by 3" (5 cm by 7.5 cm) pieces of tagboard for "fish" cards (Optional—see game board directions.)
- Die or dice and game tokens
- "Swim Along with Numbers" game directions
- Rules for the "Swim Along with Numbers" Game
- "If I Could Be . . . Not Me Anymore!" activity sheet



# FISH EYES

This story shows us the wondrous sights a fish sees as it swims through the sea. The book features cutouts of fish eyes so children can count using their tactile sense as well as the visual sense. We must close our eyes and wish to be transformed into a fish, complete with scales, fins, and a fish tail, in order to be able to navigate through the water as a fish does. We are soon swimming along with some beautiful long, green fish who are looking at us with just one eye. Next are two jumping fish that look at us with just one eye each. Three fish with smiles and four fish with stripes of different colors then pass by us. The five fish that appear next are different from the others in that they are attractively decorated with spots. Six fantail fish glide along gracefully while seven others flip their way past and, like all of the others, stare at us with just one eye each. Eight very skinny fish swim along with room to spare, and nine flying fish position themselves in relation to one another. Ten seahorses and small fish of the same size flow by on a page with beautiful blue, green, and purple hues set against a dark navy background. We complete our journey by swimming until all of the fish eyes of the different fish are looking at us on a two-page spread.

## Introduction

Before reading the story, ask students:

1. Have you ever wished you could be something else such as an animal, fish, or insect? What would you like to be? Why?
2. What is the best way to make a wish come true?
3. This story will show you what it would be like to be a fish. Would you like to be a fish? What kind?
4. What do you think you could see and do if you were a fish?

Point out that the cut–out eyes of the fish correspond to the number of fish seen each time, so that children can count in two ways.

## Mathematics Activity

Distribute "The (Fish) Eyes Have It" activity sheet to individuals or distribute one sheet to pairs or to a small group to use to record the number of fish as you reread the book. This activity provides practice in sequence counting and adding numbers 1 through 10, and may also be useful in practicing subtraction facts. Small group organization is better for the use of this book with students who need to use a tactile sense in counting, since the book can be held and the cut–out circles felt and used as counters. If you want a large group or whole-class participation, hold the book for all to see. The class can put down a corresponding counter for each fish eye shown so that they have a total to count at the end of the book. The book recommends an extension of this activity by having students count from the 10 fish back to the 1 fish, subtracting the number of fish eyes each time.

## Follow-Up Activities

The "Swim Along with Numbers" game is played by 3 to 4 players who take turns rolling a die and moving that number of spaces around the board. The first player to finish by reaching the bank and climbing out is the winner. Players are required to say, "I can move (number rolled) fish eyes," before moving or they lose a turn. Modify the play by using a pair of dice and requiring the players to add or subtract the numbers. If addition is included, the players must add the numbers on the dice and move that many spaces. If subtraction is included, the students will move the number of spaces equal to the difference of the two numbers rolled. Allow students to use counters in doing the addition and subtraction. A pattern for the game board is provided but is optional. Squares may be drawn on the file folder or tagboard piece instead of duplicating the fish pattern and gluing it on.

Stories may be created around the theme of "If I could have my wish to be a/an ______________. I would want to be a/an ______________ because ____________________." Students can choose an animal, fish, insect, or any other kind of creature they would enjoy being. Include a drawing of the subject. An effective warm-up for this activity is to ask the students to draw a picture of how they would look if they had the kind of scales, fins, and tail described in the book. Once students have a story in mind, record it on an audiotape and transcribe it later if desired. If students work best on this kind of activity in groups, the group must decide on a single choice and each member of the group should contribute a sentence or two about the things the subject will see and do as well as an individual drawing of how each would look as that creature chosen.

Such questions as the following will help students focus on just a few aspects of what will be seen and/or done after the transformation takes place:

1. What things do fish see and do that are different from what most of us see and do?
2. Can you think of anything else that a fish might be able to do and see that was not in this book? What?
3. Decide what you would like to be and think about: How you would look as (what you have chosen to be); what you would see in that different world; what you would do as that different creature

The "If I Could Be . . . Not Me Anymore!" activity sheet provides a guide for this exercise.

Name ______________________ Date ______________________

**ACTIVITY**

# THE (FISH) EYES HAVE IT

Directions: As you hear each number read in the story, use your counters or a counting frame to keep track of the fish eyes. Write the numbers on this sheet in the spaces provided.

### Total number of fish eyes looking at me:

Add every two numbers as you count them.

For example, one fish eye + (plus) two fish eyes = (equals) three fish eyes.

__________ + (plus) __________ = (equals) __________

__________ + (plus) __________ = (equals) __________

__________ + (plus) __________ = (equals) __________

__________ + (plus) __________ = (equals) __________

__________ + (plus) __________ = (equals) __________

__________ + (plus) __________ = (equals) __________

__________ + (plus) __________ = (equals) __________

__________ + (plus) __________ = (equals) __________

__________ + (plus) __________ = (equals) __________

Equals __________ fish eyes, yes, fish eyes, looking at you!!

How many fish eyes can you draw in the space below?

Name ______________________ Date ______________________

**ACTIVITY**

# DIRECTIONS FOR MAKING THE "SWIM ALONG WITH NUMBERS" GAME BOARD

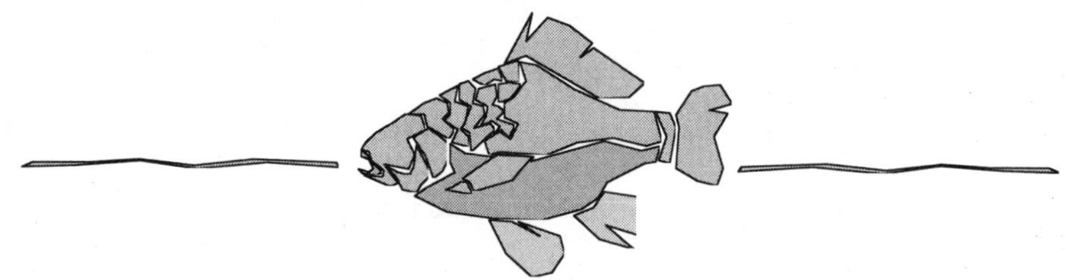

1. Duplicate the fish pattern shown about twenty times (depending on the size of the game board you want). Fish may be drawn in squares directly on the game board in a winding pattern instead.
2. If you duplicate the pattern, glue the pieces on a flattened file folder or a game-size piece of tagboard in a pattern desired. Cut two outlines of the fish with "Dive In" printed on one and "Climb Out" on the other to signify the beginning and end of the game. The game board should be laminated.
3. The background of the game board should look as much like a river as possible, for the goal of the game is to reach the far riverbank first.

Name

Date

# SWIM ALONG WITH NUMBERS GAME

### Rules Using One Die

1. Player climbing out of the river first is the winner.
2. Each player chooses a token.
3. Each player rolls the die—lowest number goes first.
4. Play moves to the right around the table.

5. Take turns rolling the die and moving the number of spaces that come up.

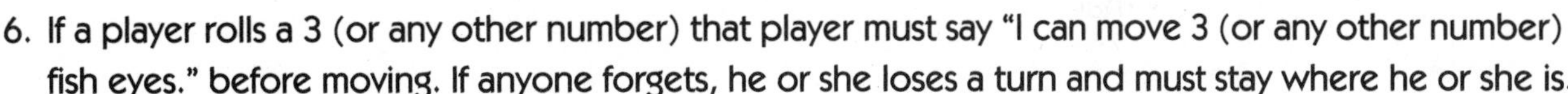

6. If a player rolls a 3 (or any other number) that player must say "I can move 3 (or any other number) fish eyes." before moving. If anyone forgets, he or she loses a turn and must stay where he or she is.

### Extra Game Rules For Addition

7. If a player rolls a 4 and a 2 (or any other combination), that player must say, "I can move 4 + 2 = 6 (or another sum) fish eyes." If the player forgets or gives the wrong answer, he or she loses the turn.

### Extra Game Rules For Subtraction

8. If a player rolls a 5 and a 3 (or any other combination) the smaller number must be subtracted from the larger and the player must say, "I can move 5 – 3 = 2 (or any other difference) fish eyes." If the player forgets or gives the wrong answer, he or she loses a turn.

Use this space for your counters.

Name ______________________ Date ______________________

**ACTIVITY**

# IF I COULD BE . . . NOT ME ANYMORE!

Directions: Think about who or what you wish to be and tell what you would see and what you would do if you were someone or something else. When you are finished, draw a picture on a separate sheet of paper showing how you would look when you are not "you" anymore.

I want to be a/an ______________________________________________

because ______________________________________________.

A way I would look different is that I ______________________________________________.

The **best** thing I would see is ______________________________________________.

The **first** thing I would do is ______________________________________________.

The best thing about being a/an ______________________________________________ is

______________________________________________

AUTHOR:
**Brian Pinkney**

STANDARD:
**Numbers and Number Sense**

CONCEPT:
**Patterns and Relationships, Computation**



# MAX FOUND TWO STICKS

Max makes good use of two sticks that have fallen off a nearby tree while he is sitting on his front steps. He taps them against his thighs to imitate the rhythm of the sound pigeons make when they fly. Then he takes possession of a bucket to make the sound of gentle raindrops hitting the windows. He beats out a tom-tom rhythm on hatboxes his mother gives him. Max places the bottles on the front fence and taps out the same rhythm made by the chimes of a nearby church. As soon as his dad leaves for work, Max grabs the garbage cans he has set out. He can beat a wonderfully loud rhythm on them that rivals the noise of the overhead train that roars past. The sudden, unexpected sound of a marching band puts a stop, but only temporarily, to Max's drumming. He is astonished to see an entire marching band turn the corner and come down his street. As soon as he recovers from his surprise, Max begins drumming again, this time in the same rhythm of the band. The last drummer spots Max and tosses him a pair of his extra drumsticks. Max doesn't waste any time dropping his sticks and catching the real ones, without even changing the rhythm of his drumming. Max breaks his silence long enough to call a thanks to the drummer for his wonderful gift.

## Introduction

As a preface to the sharing of the book, ask students if any of them take music lessons or has an older brother or sister who does. This can lead into a discussion about the different kinds of musical instruments with which they are familiar.

1. Can anyone name something you use to make music?

2. Do any of you play a musical instrument? What kind?

Explain then that this story is about a young boy who made music by using two branches that broke off a tree. Ask:

3. Can you guess what this boy did with the sticks he found?

Write the answers on the chalkboard or overhead and check them at the conclusion of the story.

## Materials:

- Rhythm sticks and other instruments from a rhythm band set—bells, maracas, tambourines, tom-toms, finger castanets, etc., so each student has something to play
- Audio or video recorder
- Music for the rhythm band performance
- "Sound Off!" activity sheet
- "Make A Match" activity sheet
- *Umbrella* by Taro Yashima (optional)

# Mathematics Activity

Before giving students any of the rhythm band instruments, discuss rhythm and beat and some examples of different rhythms demonstrated and practiced by the whole class.

As an extension, read *Umbrella* by Taro Yashima to students. They can join in the sound of the rhythm as the rain hits the umbrella as described in the text. Additional practice should consist of students responding by moving their bodies to the rhythm of the rain.

Students use rhythm band instruments to imitate the sounds and patterns made by Max with his two sticks in the "What a Band!" activity. They may choose different instruments for the sounds on each page, or all of the instruments may join in on every page. A good method is to practice with specific instruments playing each page and then join them all for a second and third play through.

The music used should be color–coded and projected on an overhead, unless it is very familiar to the students, so they will know when it is their time to join in. Any other method can be used as long as it signals to the students when they should start and stop—just pointing is a quick and effective way of giving cues. Students should practice just responding to the rhythm before attempting any songs.

After all have mastered this response. they must practice using the individual instruments assigned to each, most likely in pairs or small groups. This should precede the actual playing of the entire group, either one at a time or all together. Use songs that are familiar to the students, such as "The Wheels on the Bus" and other favorites. Make a tape recording once the group has perfected its performance.

# Follow-Up Activities

The activity sheet "Sound Off!" is used to focus student attention on particular sounds and patterns that may be heard inside and outside of school. At the conclusion of this activity, ask students to make a comparison between the sounds heard inside and the sounds heard outside. A matrix or Venn diagram will be effective in showing any commonalities.

A continued use of the rhythm band instruments is for students to imitate the sounds and patterns they hear in the immediate environment, just as Max did. This can be done inside the classroom, but it is especially effective if done both inside and outdoors, if that is possible, since it is more in keeping with the setting of the book.

The activity sheet "Make a Match" is one in which students match a person's name to the name of an instrument to complete a rhyme. For example, "Max can play the sax." for a rhyme with sax. This is a teacher–directed activity since the activity sheet must be read to the students. A transparency of the activity sheet will provide clarification by allowing students to follow along one step at a time. Names of instruments in Column Two rhyme with the names of people in Column One and students will need to listen carefully as they are read. A second reading of Column One, a sentence at a time, will help students who must copy the letter of the word in Column Two that completes the rhyme in Column One.

Name

**ACTIVITY**

Date

# SOUND OFF!

Directions: Close your eyes and listen to the sounds that you hear in the classroom or outdoors. As you hear each sound, open your eyes and write down or draw a picture of what you have heard. Check with a classmate to see if you have noticed the same sounds. Try to find at least five sounds inside and five sounds outdoors.

**Sounds That I Hear**

**INSIDE**

1.

2.

3.

4.

5.

**OUTDOORS**

1.

2.

3.

4.

5.

The same sounds we heard inside and outdoors are ______________

______________________________________________

______________________________________________

______________________________________________

Name ______________________

Date ______________________

**ACTIVITY**

# MAKE A MATCH

Directions: Listen as each column is read. Each name of a person in Column One rhymes with a name of an instrument listed in Column Two. Copy the letter in front of that name of the instrument in Column Two in the blank space provided in Column One.

**Person's Name**

1. A girl named Joan plays the slide ______________.
2. Felix Mums likes to play the ______________.
3. Nancy Nimbles really clangs the ______________.
4. Megan Scuba holds the ______________.
5. Katie Krumpet blows the ______________.
6. Bobo Niccolo is an expert on the______________.
7. Matilda Hornet plays a loud ______________.
8. Hannah Hairinet is so good with the ___________.
9. Our friend Max tootles the ______________.
10. Hector Heeder is the ______________.

**Band Instrument**

A. Cornet

B. Piccolo

C. Trumpet

D. Clarinet

E. Sax

F. Drums

G. Leader

H. Trombone

I. Cymbals

J. Tuba

How many of you can imitate the sounds of these instruments?

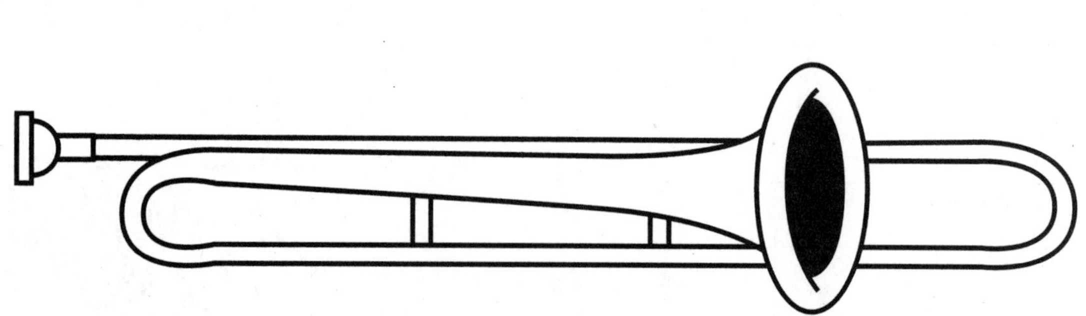

AUTHOR:
**Ed Young**

STANDARD:
**Numbers and Number Sense**

CONCEPT:
**Addition and Subtraction, Cardinal and Ordinal Numbers**

## Materials:

- A piece of tagboard with a hole cut in the middle for each pair or small group
- Pictures or photographs—one for each pair or small group
- "Where Are the Mice?" activity sheet
- "How Many Mice Are Left?" activity sheet
- "What Am I Seeing?" activity sheet
- "Number Mice" activity sheet
- 6" by 8" pieces (15 cm by 20 cm) of tagboard for each color—red, green, yellow, purple, orange, blue, and white, and for numbers—1, 2, 3, 4, 5, 6, 7, and first, second, third, fourth, fifth, sixth, seventh
- *The Book of Think,* page 39, by Marilyn Burns (optional)
- *Look Again and Take Another Look* by Tana Hoban (optional)



# SEVEN BLIND MICE

When seven blind mice discover something really strange by the pond one day, they are seized with fear and run away. The next day, a Monday, the red mouse, feeling a bit less fearful, ventures forth to try to find some clue to the identity of the thing. He feels the foot of the frightful creature and decides it is a pillar. The second mouse, the green one, sits on its trunk on Tuesday, and decides it is a great green snake. The third mouse, the yellow one, touches the tip of a tusk on Wednesday and decides he has touched a spear. On Thursday, the fourth mouse, the purple one, perches on the top of the elephant's head and believes he is on top of a tall cliff. The fifth mouse, the orange one, finds himself on the edge of a waving ear on Friday and this tells him it is a fan. On Saturday, the sixth mouse, the blue one, clings to the end of the tail and is convinced it is a rope. Sunday is the day the seventh mouse, the white one, decides to settle the identity of the creature once and for all. She runs across the "thing" in all directions and this enables her to see why each has a different opinion. Once the others explore it in the same way, they agree that it is an elephant. The lesson they all learn is that it is better to take a look at the whole picture than just one part of it if a true understanding is to be achieved.

## Introduction

After sharing this book with the students, ask the following:

1. Have you ever heard a story like this one? Tell us about it.
2. Do you think the mice would have ever convinced each other as to what the strange creature was without the help of the white mouse? Why or why not?
3. What would have happened if the white mouse had not had the idea she had?
4. What do you think the elephant thought about the mice?
5. Why do you think the author of this book changed the plot of this story by having "Seven Blind Mice" instead of the "Three Blind Mice" in the original fable? (Lead the discussion to the idea of days in the week.)

Explain to the class that they are going to act like the mice as a lead–in to the following activity.

## Mathematics Activity

Use the activity "Where Are the Mice?" to reinforce the concept of *one more, one less,* and cardinal and ordinal numbers. Give students color or number cards. When the class sings their ordinal or cardinal number or color, they stand up, move around the room, and then sit down. They will have to listen to know when their number or color of mouse is called for in the song, and remember to sit down quietly when their part is over. The number pieces will follow the pattern of the story—the first mouse, the red mouse; the second mouse, the green mouse; the third mouse, the yellow mouse; the fourth mouse, the purple mouse; the fifth mouse, the orange mouse; the sixth mouse, the blue mouse; the seventh mouse, the white mouse.

The sequence may be varied to reinforce listening skills. The song may also be sung in reverse order, requiring a minor change in the verses, for practice in subtraction skills. Another variation would be to keep each group participating until all students are circling the room in time to the song.

## Follow-Up Activities

The "How Many Mice Are Left?" activity sheet focuses on subtraction facts 0 to 7. Students are asked to determine how many mice are left in the "mice tower" when certain mice leave to explore the elephant. They must understand that they will not be counting the mice who have already explored the elephant and are off to one side in the pictures. Since accuracy depends upon the use of the book, this works best when students are paired or placed in small groups.

"Number Mice" is another fun activity. Show an example to the class of how a number can be used to take on the features of a mouse. Any part of the mouse may be shown—whole body, face, side view of head—calling for pure creativity on the part of the artist. Students may work in pairs or groups on this activity, and results should be posted on a bulletin board entitled "Magic Number Mice."

LANGUAGE

Cover pictures, photographs, or designs with a sheet of tagboard that has a small hole cut in it so that only a small part of the picture can be seen. Ask students to look at the portion of the picture or design showing through the cut–out and to identify what can be seen in the entire picture.

An example of this type of activity can be seen in *Look Again and Take a Second Look* by Tana Hoban and on page 39 of *The Book of Think* by Marilyn Burns.

Any book illustration or picture may be used as long as it is large enough so that a small section may be shown. Using designs or patterns or animal pictures is also effective. Record guesses on the "What Am I Seeing?" activity sheet.

Name

Date

# WHERE ARE THE MICE?

Directions: We are going to sing these words to the tune of "Three Blind Mice." When you hear the cardinal or ordinal number or name of the color that is on the card, you have to stand up, walk around the room in a circle, then sit down—being just as quiet as MICE!

Where are the mice? Where are the mice?
I see one, I see one.
The one that I see is the very first one,
His number is one, and his color is red,
His number is one, and his color is red,
There is the mouse. There is the mouse.

Where are the mice? Where are the mice?
There's another one, there's another one.
The one that I see is the second one,
His number is two, and his color is green,
His number is two, and his color is green,
There are the mice. There are the mice.

Where are the mice? Where are the mice?
There's another one, there's another one.
The one that I see is the very third one,
His number is three, and his color is yellow,
His number is three, and his color is yellow,
There are the mice. There are the mice.

Where are the mice? Where are the mice?
There's another one, there's another one.
The one that I see is the very fourth one,
His number is four, and his color is purple,
His number is four, and his color is purple,
There are the mice. There are the mice.

Where are the mice? Where are the mice?
There's another one, there's another one.
The one that I see is the very fifth one,
His number is five, and his color is orange,
His number is five, and his color is orange,
There are the mice. There are the mice.

Were are the mice? Where are the mice?
There's another one, there's another one.
The one that I see is the very sixth one,
His number is six, and his color is blue,
His number is six, and his color is blue,
There are the mice. There are the mice.

Where are the mice? Where are the mice?
There's another one, there's another one.
The one that I see is the very last one,
Her number is seven, and her color is white,
Her number is seven, and her color is white,
That's all the mice. That's all the mice.

| First | One | Red |
|---|---|---|
| Second | Two | Green |
| Third | Three | Yellow |
| Fourth | Four | Purple |
| Fifth | Five | Orange |
| Sixth | Six | Blue |
| Seventh | Seven | White |

Name

**ACTIVITY**

Date

# HOW MANY MICE ARE LEFT?

Directions: Think about the colors of the mice and their numbers. Write a number sentence telling how many mice are left after each number mouse has gone off to explore the elephant. Draw a picture that shows the number sentence. The first problem is done for you.

| **Number of Mouse Exploring** | | **Number Sentence of Mice Left** |
|---|---|---|
| 1. red mouse |  | 7 – 1 = 6 |
| 2. purple mouse | | |
| 3. white mouse | | |
| 4. blue mouse | | |
| 5. orange mouse | | |
| 6. yellow mouse | | |
| 7. green mouse | | |

| | |
|---|---|
| **Red Mouse's number is 1.** | **Orange Mouse's number is 5.** |
| **Green Mouse's number is 2.** | **Blue Mouse's number is 6.** |
| **Yellow Mouse's number is 3.** | **White Mouse's number is 7.** |
| **Purple Mouse's number is 4.** | |

Name

Date

**ACTIVITY**

# NUMBER MICE

Directions: Look at the numbers on this page and imagine how each might look if it were a mouse. Try to use **seven** of these numbers to make the shape of a mouse like the ones in *Seven Blind Mice*. Numbers may be turned upside down or in either direction sideways. Name each mouse if you wish.

1 2 3 4 5

6 7 8 9 10

Name ______________________ Date ______________________

ACTIVITY

# WHAT AM I SEEING?

Directions: Guess what each picture will be when you can see all of it. Tell why you think it is what you have said it is.

Picture one ______________________________________________

because ______________________________________________.

Picture two ______________________________________________

because ______________________________________________.

Picture three ______________________________________________

because ______________________________________________.

My favorite picture is ______________________________________________

because ______________________________________________.



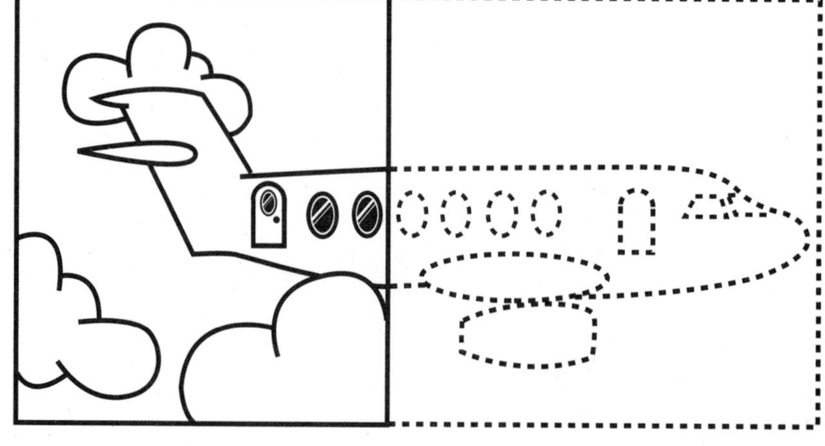

AUTHOR:

**Joseph Low**

STANDARD:

**Measurement, Estimation**

CONCEPT:

**Making Size Comparisons, Graphs**



## Materials:

- "Big and Little" activity sheet
- "A Character Study" activity sheet
- "If I were the Size of. . . " activity sheet
- Cuisenaire® rods or tiles
- Centimeter graph paper
- Crayons or markers
- Transparency of graphs
- *Once a Mouse* by Marcia Brown (optional extension activity)

# MICE TWICE

A very hungry cat invites Mouse to his home for dinner the next night. Mouse, who has known Cat and his ways for some time, accepts on the condition she be allowed to bring a friend. Cat, delighted at his vision of "mice twice," agrees. The appearance of Mouse's friend, Dog, surprises and shocks Cat. Dog's presence saves Mouse from becoming dinner that night. Dog invites Cat to dine at his house the next night, and he accepts on the condition that he may bring a friend. Cat has a surprise of his own in mind and arrives with Wolf. When Dog opens the door and reveals his friend Crocodile, they make an excuse to leave right away. Cat does, however, invite Dog and Crocodile to his house for dinner the next night, saying he wants them to meet a distant relative of his. Dog accepts, but says he will have to bring Mouse because Crocodile has to return home that night. Cat's distant relative is a huge and hungry Lion. Cat prepares a lot of good food for his dinner guests to eat before they are eaten, and he and Lion await their arrival in anticipation of a wonderful meal for themselves. However, Cat is outsmarted once again, as Dog and Mouse bring their friend Wasp. Wasp stings Lion immediately. Lion runs off, followed by Cat, who is pursued by Dog. Wasp and Mouse sample the delicious food, leaving some for Dog in case he doesn't catch up with Cat.

## Introduction

Before reading the story to the class, show children the cover picture and ask the following questions:

1. Can you tell from the picture what the story is about?
2. What do you think the title means?
3. How many mice would be "Mice Twice"? "Mice Thrice?"
4. Why do you think cats and mice are enemies?
5. Do you think that cats have other enemies? Who are they?
6. Can cats be nice? "Nice Twice?" "Nice Thrice?"

Record predictions on the chalkboard or an overhead transparency to review at the conclusion of the reading. Share the story and then discuss the differences in size and characteristics of the various animals with such questions as:

1. Did Cat get away from Dog?
2. Do you think Cat and Lion will be friends anymore? Why or why not?

3. Was it just as wrong for Cat to want to eat Mouse as it was of Dog to want Cat? Explain your answer.
4. Who was the most clever character in the story? How do you know this?
5. Why was it possible for the smallest character, Wasp, to defeat the largest character, Lion? Could this happen with human characters? Why or why not?
6. What did you notice about the time set for dinner each night? Why do you suppose this happened?
7. Do you know any other stories like this?
8. What do you think would have happened if Dog had not had Crocodile at his house and instead had Mouse when Cat brought Wolf?

## Mathematics Activity

The activity consists of making a comparison of the sizes of the characters using Cuisenaire® rods, graph paper, tiles, and crayons or markers. Students will follow along using their rods and graph paper in the activity "Big and Little" as you demonstrate on the overhead. Guidelines for the students are:

1. Look at the picture of Mouse and Cat together as Dog and Mouse stand in the doorway of Cat's house and estimate of how much larger Cat is than Mouse.
2. Compare your estimate with that of a classmate.
3. Look at your paper and circle the number that is closest to your estimate of the size difference.
4. Follow along on your paper as you listen to the directions for using your Cuisenaire® rods to show the size differences among all of the animals.

Students should then place the smallest number of rods (if they are using them) tiles. or whatever manipulative materials are being used, on the centimeter or graph paper. They are to draw an outline around the rods they use with crayon or marker. These graphs can be shown to classmates. Then, in pairs or small groups, students should compare their results to see if everyone agrees on the rods used.

## Follow-Up Activities

Take a poll of the students to determine if there is one character in the story the majority like best. Each will fill in the first part of the "A Character Study" activity sheet as you read to them. Then combine all choices on an overhead transparency. Take a second poll in which students decide which character they would prefer to be if they were in this story. Follow the same procedure to produce a second graph on the overhead so comparisons can be made on the two graphs and of the choices. Guideline questions may include:

1. How many of you chose–Wasp–Mouse–Cat–Dog–Wolf–Crocodile–Lion as your favorite character? Look at the graph to see.
2. How many of you chose–Wasp–Mouse–Cat–Dog–Wolf–Crocodile–Lion–as the character you would like to be if you were in this story? Look at the graph to see.

To extend this activity, read *Once a Mouse* by Marcia Brown. After you share this book, use the following questions to generate a discussion about *big* and *little* and the similarities between the two stories:

1. Does anyone see some way that these two stories are alike? How?
2. Are there any characters that are alike in the two books? Which are they? How are they alike?
3. Do you have a favorite character in *Once a Mouse*? Which is it?
4. Did the character who was first a mouse become nicer and more considerate as he grew so much bigger?
5. Do you think that size is the only consideration in how much a person can accomplish or how effective in helping others he/she can be? Explain your answer.

# Follow-Up Activities Con't.

An additional extension activity is to have students bring in empty commercial product cartons such as those for soap, toothpaste, and laundry powders to continue making size comparisons. For example, what is the difference between small and medium sized? Medium and large? Large and extra large? Extra large and giant size?

A poem entitled "I'm Tired of Being Little" in *Something Big Has Been Here* by Jack Prelutsky is perfect to use to finish this activity and lead into the follow-up language activity.

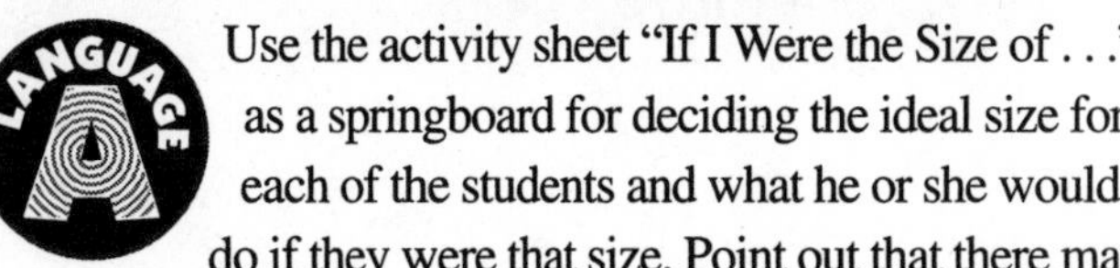


Use the activity sheet "If I Were the Size of . . ." as a springboard for deciding the ideal size for each of the students and what he or she would do if they were that size. Point out that there may be some advantages to the students in being smaller instead of bigger and that they should think about which would be the best size change for each of them. They also need to think of the size of an object or other person which would be their ideal size. Have them draw a picture at the bottom of the page showing one of the actions the students would take if he or she were a different size.

Name ____________________ Date ____________________

**ACTIVITY**

# BIG AND LITTLE

20 ____________________

18 ____________________

16 ____________________

14 ____________________

12 ____________________

10 ____________________

8 ____________________

6 ____________________

4 ____________________

2 ____________________

0 ____________________

**WASP** **MOUSE** **CAT** **DOG** **WOLF** **CROCODILE** **LION**

1. Circle the number of times that Cat is bigger than Mouse. 2 4 6 8 12 14
2. Use the white Cuisenaire® rod to show the size of Mouse. What rod will show the size of Cat? Trace around each rod you use on the graph above.
3. If the red rod shows the size of Mouse, what rod will show the size of Cat? Trace them.
4. How many ways can you think of to show the difference in sizes among these animals?
5. Can you show the difference on this graph between the size of Wasp and that of Lion? Why or why not?

Name ____________________ Date ____________________

**ACTIVITY**

# CENTIMETER GRAPH PAPER

Directions: Using your Cuisenaire® rods, show ways of making the comparisons of the sizes of Wasp, Mouse, Cat, Dog, Wolf, Crocodile, and Lion that you were asked to do on the "Big and Little" page.

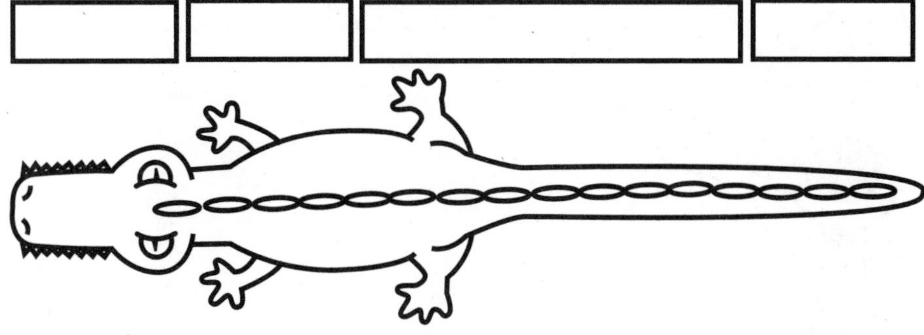

Name ______________________ Date ______________________

**ACTIVITY**

# A CHARACTER STUDY

Directions: Decide which of the characters in the story *Mice Twice* you liked the most and explain why by completing the sentences on the first half of this page. Decide then which of the characters you would like to be if you were in this story and explain that choice by completing the sentences on the lower half of the page.

## My Favorite Character

The character I liked best is ______________ because he/she ______________________________

__________________________________________________________________________

and the others in the story ______________________________________________________

__________________________________________________________________________

If I could change what happened to this character in any way it would be for him/her to __________

__________________________________________________________________________

__________________________________________________________________________

## The Character I Would Like to Be

The character I would be in this story is ____________ because he/she ____________________

__________________________________________________________________________

while the others in the story just __________________________________________________

__________________________________________________________________________

One thing I would do differently in the story if I were in it is ______________________________

because ______________________________________________________

__________________________________________________________________

__________________________________________________________________

Name

Date

ACTIVITY

# IF I WERE THE SIZE OF . . .

I want to be as (big) (little) as ____________________

____________________

because ____________________.

I would look ____________________.

I would say no when ____________________.

I could help ____________________

and could go ____________________

and have ____________________.

This is a picture of me when I am a different size.

AUTHOR:
**Molly Bang**

STANDARD:
**Patterns and Relationships, Estimation**

CONCEPT:
**Size Comparisons**

## Materials:

- Color tiles or pattern blocks
- "Patterns Here, Patterns There" activity sheet
- "How Accurate Are Your Predictions?" activity sheet
- "Find the Hidden Words" activity sheet
- 4 different-sized jars or containers for each small group
- A variety of materials such as jelly beans, spice drops, unpopped corn, or beans for each group
- A balance scale available for each group's use

# THE GREY LADY AND THE STRAWBERRY SNATCHER

**The Grey Lady buys some delicious-looking strawberries at the market and begins to walk home with them, unaware that she is being followed by the sinister Strawberry Snatcher, who also wants those strawberries. When she realizes he is following her, she becomes alarmed and begins to run from him. In her panic, she doesn't notice a snake charmer on a skateboard coming from the other direction, and she crashes into her. The Snatcher grabs the skateboard and uses it to gain some speed in his pursuit of the Grey Lady as she boards a bus. She leaves it to walk through a misty, swamp-like area with the Snatcher right behind her. He nearly catches up with her several times, but she always manages to elude him. Just as he thinks he has her cornered, she swings out over his head on a rope-like branch and drops down at the edge of the trees. The Snatcher is quick, though, and is almost within arm's reach of the strawberries when she just disappears. He looks in all directions but she has simply vanished. What he does see is a large clump of blackberry bushes loaded with fruit. He tastes the blackberries and decides that they will be a good substitute for the strawberries. The Grey Lady arrives home safely with the precious strawberries intact, much to her family's delight.**

## Introduction

Talk to the students about their favorite fruits, leading into the idea that the book they are going to look at is about two people who really love strawberries and what happens when they both want the same basket of strawberries. Ask if they have ever had something like that happen to them, and use the following questions to generate their comments:

1. Have you and someone else ever wanted the very same thing? What?
2. How did you decide which of you got it?
3. Were both of you happy about it? Why or why not?
4. Do you think that the way it was decided was fair? Why or why not?

It is best to share the book with small groups since the story is fully dependent on seeing all of the details in the illustrations. If there is a fiber-optics room in your school, show the book on the overhead projector there. It is an ideal way for everyone to see it at the same time.

Ask the following questions once the book has been shared:

1. What do you think about the Strawberry Snatcher?
2. What do you think would have happened if the blackberry bushes had not been there for the Strawberry Snatcher to enjoy?
3. Why do you think the Strawberry Snatcher wanted that particular basket of strawberries?
4. Why do you suppose the Grey Lady didn't pick blackberries for her family instead of going to the fruit store to buy strawberries?
5. Did the Strawberry Snatcher deserve the blackberries? Why or why not?
6. There are five people in the Grey Lady's family. Do you think each person was able to eat his/her fill of the strawberries? Why or why not?
7. Do you like strawberries? Could you eat a whole basket of them by yourself?

## Mathematics Activity

Use the activity sheet "Patterns Here, Patterns There" to bring out the many patterns in the book's illustrations. After the initial sharing, show the book again to small groups in order to direct attention to the patterns in the sidewalk, in the window panes, in the window displays, and so on. Hold a discussion about objects in the classroom that show patterns as well. Ask students to duplicate some of these patterns with blocks or tiles either working alone, in pairs, or in groups of four. Give them a chance to create their own patterns. Show individual patterns on the overhead for the whole class to duplicate.

## Follow-Up Activities

The book makes an assumption that the strawberries bought by the Grey Lady were in a quart basket. Hold a short discussion about how different kinds of containers are needed for different kinds of food.

1. Have any of you seen strawberries at the market in baskets like the one the Grey Lady carried?
2. Why do you suppose that different kinds of food come in different kinds of packages? For example, what would happen if a quart of milk were packaged in a basket like this?
3. Do you think that a quart basket like the strawberry basket will hold more jumbo marshmallows or more jelly beans? How can you find out?

Students should work in small groups using the activity sheet "How Accurate Are Your Predictions?" to predict and record how many pieces of each of the materials will be needed to fill the different-sized containers labeled A, B, C, and D. As each container is filled, have students record the results and compare the predictions.

An extension of this activity is to determine if the shape of the container makes a difference in the value of what is sold. After students fill each container and count pieces, they weigh the containers to determine if the number of pieces each holds influences the weight.

Using a variety of edible materials adds to the enjoyment of this activity since students can eat the materials at the end of the activity.

The activity sheet "Find the Hidden Words" requires students to take a close look at some of the words in the title of the story. Using the letters in the words "strawberry" and/or "snatcher," ask students to create as many shorter words as they can for the purpose of enriching vocabulary and practicing spelling (for example, words such as "be," "at," "bat," "straw," "berry," "rest," and so on). Set a time limit for students working individually or in small groups, or make this an ongoing challenge in an activity center or workstation.

Name Date

ACTIVITY

# PATTERNS HERE, PATTERNS THERE

Directions: Look at the book *The Grey Lady and the Strawberry Snatcher* again and notice how many different patterns there are in the illustrations. Use your color tiles or pattern block pieces to try to make one of these patterns. Trace around the pattern you made before going on to the next part. For example, a brick sidewalk is shown in one of the illustrations. Make a small part of that sidewalk. Look around the classroom to find another pattern and make a part of it. Then make up a pattern of your own.

1. Some of the patterns I see are ______________________

______________________________________

______________________________________

2. This is a pattern I can copy.

3. This is a copy of a pattern I see in the classroom.

4. This is my own pattern.

Name

Date

# HOW ACCURATE ARE YOUR PREDICTIONS?

Directions: There are four different-sized containers and four different kinds of materials with which to fill them. Guess how many pieces each container will hold and write that number in the blanks in the first table. Then fill each container, counting the pieces as you do, and write that number in the blanks in the second table. Compare the numbers to see how good your guesses were.

| Container | Materials—Estimate | | | |
|---|---|---|---|---|
| | 1 | 2 | 3 | 4 |
| A | | | | |
| B | | | | |
| C | | | | |
| D | | | | |

| Container | Materials—Actual | | | |
|---|---|---|---|---|
| | 1 | 2 | 3 | 4 |
| A | | | | |
| B | | | | |
| C | | | | |
| D | | | | |

**My predictions were: (circle one)**

not very close

a few were close

most were close

all were exactly right

Name ______________________ Date ______________________

**ACTIVITY**

# FIND THE HIDDEN WORDS

Directions: Look for the shorter two-, three-, four-, and five-letter words hidden in two of the words included in the title of this book, "strawberry" and "snatcher." Find as many as you can in the time provided. When you are finished, compare your list with the lists others have made to see if you found some of the same words.

**STRAWBERRY**

| Two-letter words | Three-letter words | Four-letter words | More letters than four |
|---|---|---|---|
| ______ | ______ | ______ | ______ |
| ______ | ______ | ______ | ______ |
| ______ | ______ | ______ | ______ |
| ______ | ______ | ______ | ______ |
| ______ | ______ | ______ | ______ |

**SNATCHER**

| Two-letter words | Three-letter words | Four-letter words | More letters than four |
|---|---|---|---|
| ______ | ______ | ______ | ______ |
| ______ | ______ | ______ | ______ |
| ______ | ______ | ______ | ______ |
| ______ | ______ | ______ | ______ |
| ______ | ______ | ______ | ______ |

**Total Number of Words With:**

two letters ______ three letters ______ four letters ______ more than four ______

**Total Number of All Words:** ______________

AUTHOR:

**Arnold Lobel**

STANDARD:

**Problem Solving, Estimation**

CONCEPT:

**Numbers and Number Sense**

## Materials:

- "My Number Garden" activity sheet
- "Who Is Really The Greatest?" activity sheet
- "Cookie Cooking Counting" activity sheet
- "My Own Toad List" activity sheet
- Calculators
- Measuring spoons and cups



# FROG AND TOAD TOGETHER

Five separate stories detail the adventures these two friends have together in this easy-to-read book.

"The List" begins as Toad wakes up and decides to make a list of things to do that day. He shows his list to Frog when the two go for a walk together. The wind blows the list away from Toad, leaving Frog to try to catch it, but he cannot. The two just have to sit and do nothing, since Toad cannot remember the items on the list. Finally, when Frog says it is time to go home to sleep, Toad remembers that "go to sleep" is on the list, so that is what they do.

"The Garden" tells what happens when Frog gives Toad some seeds so he can have a garden of his own like Frog's. Toad plants them and then is worried when they do not grow immediately. He reads stories and poems to them, sings songs, and plays music to them, so they will not be afraid to grow. He becomes so tired after all this work that he falls asleep in the garden. Frog has to wake him up to show him that the seeds have sprouted.

"The Cookies" relates how difficult it is to resist temptation. Toad's freshly baked cookies taste so good that Frog and Toad cannot stop eating them. They decide to put them on a high shelf where they cannot reach them, but they know they will try. Frog reaches the only solution possible—he takes the cookies outside and gives them to the birds. Toad goes home to bake a cake!

"Dragons and Giants" find Frog and Toad trying to prove that they are brave. They climb a mountain, run from an avalanche, encounter and escape a hungry snake in a cave, and are threatened by a hawk who is looking for a meal. All through this, they keep repeating that they are brave! They run all the way back to Toad's house where, after complimenting each other on their bravery, Toad hides under the bed covers and Frog locks himself in the closet.

"The Dream" involves Toad in a scary nightmare. He dreams that as he is becoming more and more talented and famous, Frog is becoming smaller and unimportant. A strange voice introduces him as the most wonderful Toad in the world while he demonstrates his many accomplishments—playing the piano without making a single mistake, balancing on the high wire, and dancing. By then Frog has grown so small and

**insignificant that he cannot even be seen. Toad screams for Frog to come back and wakes himself up. Frog is standing by his bed and is his own right size. Toad is assured that he has not harmed his friend and the two plan to have a good breakfast and a wonderful day together.**

## Introduction

Read individual episodes or the entire book to the children and then hold a discussion. It is a book that many students are capable of reading on their own and is excellent to use for peer reading. There are many ideas presented about friendship; emphasize those by asking the following before reading the book, and again after the book is finished:

1. Why do you think that Frog and Toad are such good friends?
2. Do friends look after each other? When? How?
3. Should friends have fun together?
4. How fast do seeds grow once they are planted?
5. Have you ever tasted anything so good that it was hard to stop eating it? What?
6. What do people do to show they are brave? What do you think Frog and Toad will do to show how brave they are?
7. Have you ever had a nightmare? Are nightmares really scary? How can someone get over being upset by a nightmare?

## Mathematics Activity

The "My Number Garden" activity sheet for the practice of addition and/or subtraction facts allows students to "plant" two numbers that will "flower" into one number bloom. For example, if they plant 3 and 2, 4 and 1, or 0 and 5, the bloom will be 5. They may have several of the same number bloom from different seeds they have chosen to plant. For subtraction, the number planted may be 10 and 8, 6 and 4, 9 and 7, 8 and 6, etc., and the number bloom is 2. When the plants and flowers are all flourishing, students may add color to them.

## Follow-Up Activities

The "Who Is Really the Greatest?" activity provides additional experience in counting using a hundreds chart. To find the number needed on the chart, students begin counting at the number mentioned. If they have done all the problems correctly, they will discover who the greatest is! Work on this sheet is best done in pairs or cooperative groups.

The "Cookie Cooking Counting" activity sheet requires students to adapt a cookie recipe so that there will be enough for twice as many servings as provided in the recipe. Students may need to use calculators to do the computations.

LANGUAGE

Remind students of the list that Toad made to help him remember the things he wanted to do one day. These questions will help focus on the idea of making lists.

1. Was it a good idea for Toad to make a list? Why or why not?
2. Do you ever forget to do some things you are supposed to do? When?
3. Does anyone in your family make lists? Who makes the list and what kind is it?
4. What problems could result from making a list?
5. Have you ever made a list of things you need to remember to do? Did the list keep you from forgetting to do something you should have done? What?

Tell students that they are going to have a chance to make a list like Toad's, and that they should include all of the things that they do in and out of school. A sheet of paper divided into two columns allows for a comparison of the length of each list. Students should estimate which list will be longer before they do any writing and compare that estimate after each is completed. Students may also compare their lists with others. An extension of this activity is for students to designate the things on their lists that they especially like and do not like to do.

Name ____________ Date ____________

ACTIVITY

# MY NUMBER GARDEN

Directions: Plant two number seeds and they will grow into a number flower. In addition the number flower will be the sum of your seeds. In subtraction the number flower will be the difference between the two seeds. See what kind of garden you can have.

Plant addition seeds in numbers 1 to 5 following this example.

**Example: Seed numbers 2 + 3 Flower number is 5**

1. Seed numbers _______ + _______ Flower number is _____
2. Seed numbers _______ + _______ Flower number is _____
3. Seed numbers _______ + _______ Flower number is _____
4. Seed numbers _______ + _______ Flower number is _____
5. Seed numbers _______ + _______ Flower number is _____

Plant subtraction seeds in numbers 6 to 10 following this example.

**Seed numbers 8 – 2 Flower number is 6**

6. Seed numbers _______ – _______ Flower number is _____
7. Seed numbers _______ – _______ Flower number is _____
8. Seed numbers _______ – _______ Flower number is _____
9. Seed numbers _______ – _______ Flower number is _____
10. Seed numbers _______ – _______ Flower number is _____

Draw and color a picture of your garden showing some of its beautiful flowers.

Name

Date

# WHO IS REALLY THE GREATEST?

Directions: Toad liked being called the "greatest" until he saw what it was doing to his friend, Frog. Use the hundreds chart to color in the numbers asked for at the bottom of the page and letters will be formed that will tell you who really is the "greatest."

| 1 | 2 | 3 | 4 | 5 | 6 | 7 | 8 | 9 | 10 |
|---|---|---|---|---|---|---|---|---|---|
| 11 | 12 | 13 | 14 | 15 | 16 | 17 | 18 | 19 | 20 |
| 21 | 22 | 23 | 24 | 25 | 26 | 27 | 28 | 29 | 30 |
| 31 | 32 | 33 | 34 | 35 | 36 | 37 | 38 | 39 | 40 |
| 41 | 42 | 43 | 44 | 45 | 46 | 47 | 48 | 49 | 50 |
| 51 | 52 | 53 | 54 | 55 | 56 | 57 | 58 | 59 | 60 |
| 61 | 62 | 63 | 64 | 65 | 66 | 67 | 68 | 69 | 70 |
| 71 | 72 | 73 | 74 | 75 | 76 | 77 | 78 | 79 | 80 |
| 81 | 82 | 83 | 84 | 85 | 86 | 87 | 88 | 89 | 90 |
| 91 | 92 | 93 | 94 | 95 | 96 | 97 | 98 | 99 | 100 |

Figure out which squares to color by adding or subtracting.

**First Letter:**
2 less than 13
5 more than 8
4 less than 25
8 more than 15
11 more than 20
9 less than 42
5 more than 37
3 less than 55
8 more than 54
7 less than 79

**Second Letter:**
6 more than 38
2 less than 47
5 more than 41
4 less than 58
7 less than 63
8 more than 56
6 more than 60
10 more than 64
4 less than 79
5 more than 71

**Third Letter:**
6 more than 42
5 less than 55
9 more than 49
5 more than 55
8 more than 60
7 more than 63
9 less than 87
3 less than 82
6 more than 74

______ Name

**ACTIVITY**

______ Date

# COOKIE COOKING COUNTING

Directions: You want to bake cookies for a party but there is a problem. The only recipe you can find is just for one–half as many cookies as you need. What can you do? Work with a partner or small group to determine the best way to solve this problem. Use this space to write your ideas for changing the recipe. Then fill in the blanks in the "Your Changes" column.

| **Lemon Moons** | **Your Changes** |
|---|---|
| 1 cup of flour | ______ cups of flour |
| 1 teaspoon of baking powder | ______ teaspoons of baking powder |
| 1/4 teaspoon of salt | ______ teaspoon of salt |
| pinch of nutmeg | ______ pinches of nutmeg |
| 1 egg | ______ eggs |
| 1/3 cup of cooking oil | ______ cup of cooking oil |
| 1/2 cup of sugar | ______ cup of sugar |
| 1 teaspoon of lemon peel | ______ teaspoons of lemon peel |
| 1 teaspoon of lemon juice | ______ teaspoons of lemon juice |
| | |
| 240 ml flour | ______ ml flour |
| 5 ml baking powder | ______ ml baking powder |
| 1.25 ml salt | ______ ml salt |
| pinch of nutmeg | ______ pinches of nutmeg |
| 1 egg | ______ eggs |
| 80 ml cooking oil | ______ ml cooking oil |
| 120 ml sugar | ______ ml sugar |
| 5 ml lemon peel | ______ ml lemon peel |
| 5 ml lemon juice | ______ ml lemon juice |

Preheat oven to 400°F. (105°C). Mix flour, baking powder, salt, and nutmeg in one bowl. Use another bowl to mix the rest of the ingredients and add them to the first bowl. Drop by tablespoons onto a greased cookie sheet and bake for 8 minutes.

Name

Date

# MY OWN TOAD LIST

**School Day List** | **Saturday List**

1. ______ ______
2. ______ ______
3. ______ ______
4. ______ ______
5. ______ ______
6. ______ ______
7. ______ ______
8. ______ ______
9. ______ ______
10. ______ ______
11. ______ ______
12. ______ ______

Choose one activity from each list that you like to do best and explain why you like it. ______

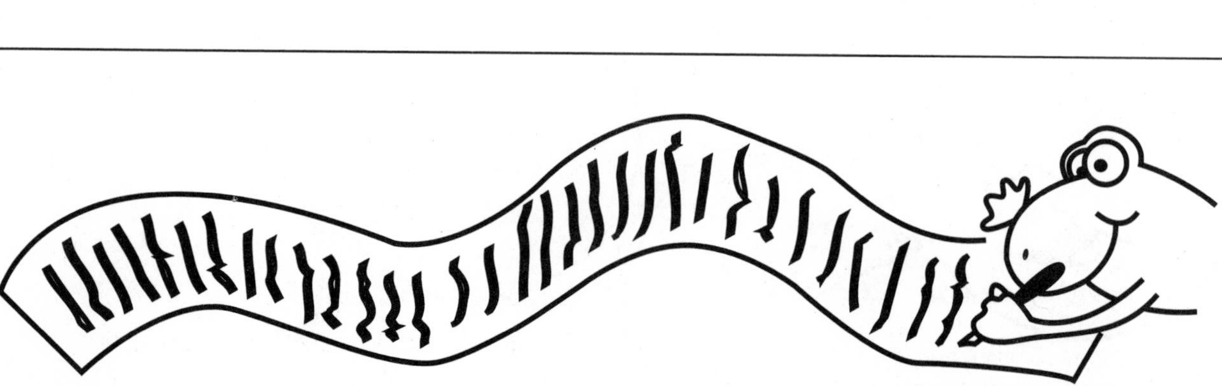

AUTHOR:

**James Marshall**

STANDARD:

**Patterns and Relationships, Problem Solving**

CONCEPT:

**Whole Number Operations, Sequences**

## Materials:

- "Follow the Pattern" activity sheet
- Transparency of the "Follow the Pattern" activity sheet
- "Folktale Numbers—Lucky or Not?" activity sheet
- "Advice from ______________" activity sheet
- Tagboard strips with sentences or actions from the story (optional)
- Masking tape or magnets for attaching the strips to the chalkboard (optional)
- Audio recorder (optional)

# GOLDILOCKS AND THE THREE BEARS

**This Goldilocks is the kind of child that most people would avoid at any costs. Her mother warns her not to take the short cut through the forest as she leaves on an errand. She promises readily enough, but the minute she is out of her mother's sight, she heads straight for the short cut. She ignores the many warning signs and forges ahead. The bears who live in a nice little house in the forest have gone for a ride on their bicycle while their porridge cools. Goldilocks walks in the unlocked door and goes through the familiar routine of eating Baby Bear's porridge, breaking his chair, and falling asleep in his bed. When the bears come home and see all of the damage she has done, they become very upset. Baby Bear comes out the worst because he finds that the someone who has been in his bed is still in it, sound asleep! Goldilocks wakes up when Papa Bear roars in anger, and, without wasting a moment, leaps out of the window and runs off. The bears never find out the identity of their visitor, but they do know they never want her to come back, and as far as we know, she never has. Marshall adds a number of interesting details in the illustrations that enrich the story and add much humor to this refreshing new version of a well-loved story.**

## Introduction

Ask the following questions before reading the story:

1. How many of you have heard the story of Goldilocks and the Three Bears?
2. Could you tell what kind of girl Goldilocks was from the story?
3. What was she like?
4. Did she do anything she should not have done? What?

Once the students have shared some ideas, explain that this author, James Marshall, portrays Goldilocks in a different light from the way she is pictured in many other versions, and/or in the way they may have envisioned her. After sharing the story, ask:

1. Does anyone see a way in which this Goldilocks is a little different from those in other stories?
2. What is one difference?
3. Do you like this Goldilocks? Why or why not?
4. Is this Goldilocks someone you would enjoy having as a friend? Why or why not? What kinds of things might you two do together?
5. Name two things Goldilocks did that she should not have done.

Allow a brief discussion, and then lead into one of the activities.

## Mathematics Activity

The "Follow the Pattern" activity sheet requires students to place the various events and actions in the story in the proper sequence by listening to you read each statement and then numbering the statements in the order in which each happened in the story. It must be made clear to students that they are to number the first thing that happened as number "1," the second as number "2," and so forth. If this is used as a whole-class activity, students may fill in the transparency. For a chalkboard activity, use strips of tagboard with those events or specific actions printed on them. Magnets attached to the back of the strips or pieces of masking tape will make them adhere to the chalkboard, and students can come to the board in turn and put them in the proper sequence. For a variation, give one strip to each of 13 students and have them line up in the order of the sequence of events, or just have them line up and allow those seated to tell them where to stand.

## Follow-Up Activities

"Folktale Numbers—Lucky or Not?" focuses on the so-called magical numbers of 3 and 7, among others, that appear so often in these stories. Students must discover different ways of making these combinations using addition and subtraction skills. Ask them what they think their lucky numbers are.

LANGUAGE

Students may use the "Advice from ______________" activity sheet as a guide for writing a letter to Goldilocks or any other favorite folktale character, giving advice on how to solve any problems or to say what the character should have done to stay away from trouble in the original story. Each may make an audiotape of his or her letter instead of putting it on paper.

An extension activity is for pairs or small groups to act out a scene in which they tell the character exactly what the character did wrong or what they liked about what the character did.

These activities and this book are excellent for studying the various types of traditional literature and for exploring the differences in the illustrator's interpretation of a particular story.

Name

Date

**ACTIVITY**

# FOLLOW THE PATTERN

Directions: Follow the pattern of Goldilocks's story. Listen to the sentences, then write a number–1 for the first thing that happens to 13, for the last thing that happens—in the blanks to show the order in which the events took place in the story. Work with a partner or group to find the answers.

_____ Goldilocks walks into the house of the Bears.

_____ The Bear family goes for a ride on their bicycle.

_____ Goldilocks's mother tells her not to take the short cut.

_____ Goldilocks falls asleep in Baby Bear's bed.

_____ Papa Bear tastes the porridge and says it is too hot.

_____ Goldilocks smashes Baby Bear's chair.

_____ The Bear family returns to the house.

_____ Goldilocks jumps out the window.

_____ Papa Bear says that someone has been sitting in his chair.

_____ Baby Bear discovers Goldilocks in his bed.

_____ Goldilocks eats the porridge.

_____ Goldilocks takes the short cut.

_____ Goldilocks did not hear the bears come home.

How could you find out from this list how many different things happen in this story?

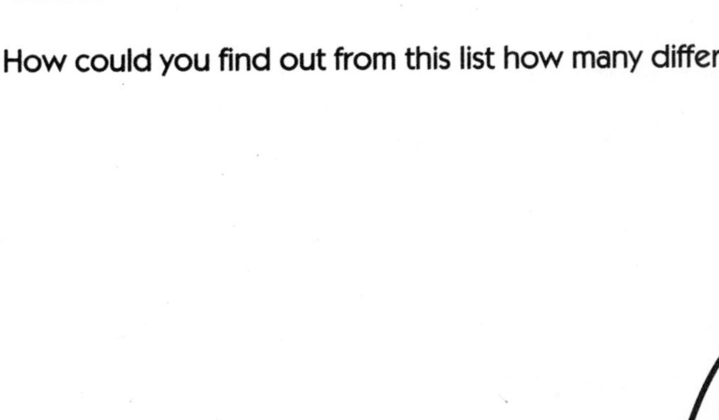

Name

Date

# FOLKTALE NUMBERS—LUCKY OR NOT?

Directions: Numbers appear very often in the titles of folktales or in the action during the story. Some of the titles of these tales are listed below but the numbers are missing. Look at the clues. Then fill in those missing numbers. Use your calculator if you need some help in finding the numbers.

| | | |
|---|---|---|
| 1. The Story of the _____ Little Pigs | (Clue: 14 – 13 + 2) | 4 points |
| 2. Goldilocks and the _____ Bears | (Clue: 10 – 8 + 1) | 4 points |
| 3. Snow White and the _____ Dwarfs | (Clue: 5 + 6 – 4) | 4 points |
| 4. The Story of the _____ Ravens | (Clue: 20 + 6 – 19) | 4 points |
| 5. The _____ Billy Goats Gruff | (Clue: 15 – 14 + 2) | 4 points |
| 6. The Wolf and the _____ Kids | (Clue: 18 – 12 + 1) | 4 points |
| 7. The Miller and His _____ Sons | (Clue: 9 + 9 – 14) | 4 points |
| 8. _____ –Eye, _____ –Eyes, _____ –Eyes | (Clue: each number is 1 more than the last and the middle number is 2) | 8 points |
| 9. The _____ Dancing Princesses | (Clue: 5 + 5 + 5 – 3) | 4 points |
| 10. The Boy of the _____ -Year Nap | (Clue: 4 + 4 – 5) | 4 points |
| 11. The _____ Chinese Brothers | (Clue: 16 – 12 + 3) | 4 points |
| 12. Ali Baba and the _____ Thieves | (Clue: 10 added four times) | Bonus 12 points |

**Add your number of points. 60 points are possible.**

52 to 60 points—super!

40 to 48 points—you know your facts!

28 to 36 points—not bad!

Fewer points—read more folktales!

Name

Date

# ADVICE FROM ________________________

Directions: Fill in the blanks by writing a letter to Goldilocks or another folktale character. Give this character some advice on how to avoid getting into trouble or on how to get out of trouble once they are in it. You can let this character in on what always works for you—unless you never get into trouble!

To ____________________ Date ____________________

At ____________________

____________________

Dear ____________________

What I think you should do is ________________________________________

____________________________________________________________

____________________________________________________________

____________________________________________________________

____________________________________________________________

____________________________________________________________

Please write and tell me if my advice has helped you.

Sincerely,

____________________

(Official Advice Columnist)

AUTHOR:

**David Wiesner**

STANDARD:

**Number Sense, Mathematics as Communication**

CONCEPT:

**Addition and Subtraction**

## Materials:

- "The Lucky(?) Seven" activity sheet
- Directions for constructing the "How Many Matches Can You Make?" game
- "How Many Matches Can You Make?" game sheet
- "Is Tuesday Really Your Favorite Day?" activity sheet
- 20 to 26 pieces of 2" by 3" (5 cm by 7.5 cm) tagboard, twelve of one color, the rest of another color, laminated
- Calculators

# TUESDAY

**This nearly wordless book clearly describes the strange happenings on a normally quiet weekday night. A fleet of rather self-satisfied, smug-looking frogs are shown flying high in the sky on lily pads. Some of them experiment with this new sensation of flying by trying out daring loops, others delight in frightening birds off telephone wires, and others just stare ahead fixedly, intent on what may be coming. A man having a late snack in his kitchen averts his eyes to avoid seeing what he thinks he is seeing as they swoop down beside his window. They cross a backyard and one of them captures a tablecloth off the clothesline to use as a sail. They zoom into another house where the occupant has fallen asleep while watching late-night television. They settle in to watch a show or two. They leave at 4:00 a.m., and one of them, flying a bit too low, encounters a hostile dog who takes a bite out of the lily pad. This destroys its power to sustain flight. Even though the other frogs gather and drive the dog off, they cannot stay aloft for all of the lily pads are collapsing. The police, the emergency crews, and the media people are mystified by the appearance of so many lily pads littering the street at dawn. The mystery soon dies down and all seems to return to normal again—until the following Tuesday night, when the sky is filled with flying pigs!**

## Introduction

Before sharing the book, lead into it by talking about the days of the week and asking such questions as:

1. How many days are in a week?
2. Does anyone have a favorite day?
3. What makes a day your favorite one?

Introduce the book by reading the title. Explain that students must look at the illustrations closely to understand the story. After sharing the book, ask:

1. Do you think what happened in this book could happen in our world?
2. Has anyone ever heard of flying saucers? When?
3. Might people looking up into the sky at night mistake the flying frogs or pigs for a flying saucer? Why or why not?

Remind students of the difference between "make–believe" fantasy stories and the stories in realistic literature which may really happen in the world we know. Then introduce one of the activities.

## Mathematics Activity

The activity sheet "The Lucky(?) Seven" focuses on the following coincidences connected with the book:

- The title, *Tuesday,* consists of seven letters
- The author's last name, Wiesner, has seven letters in it
- The name of the publishing company, Clarion, has seven letters in it

This generates the question of how significant the number seven can be. This is certainly u–n–u–s–u–a–l, if not s–t–r–a–n–g–e! Present shorter words formed from "Tuesday" and give the letters the number values as shown on touch-tone telephone buttons. When students copy these values and add them together, they will see that seven appears in every word, either in the individual values or the sum. For example, "Tuesday" has the letter values of $8 + 8 + 3 + 7 + 3 + 2 + 9$ and equals 40; Weisner, the letter values of $9 + 3 + 4 + 7 + 4 + 3 + 7 = 37$. Showing this "coincidence" to the class before the activity begins may generate a whole-class discussion. You can also accomplish this in a post–activity discussion to determine what conclusions they reached in doing this activity.

## Follow-Up Activities

"How Many Matches Can You Make?" is a card game to extend the skills of recognizing equivalent addition and subtraction equations. Make a set of twelve addition facts and eight subtraction facts printed on tagboard cards. Use one color for the addition facts and a different color for subtraction facts. Additional subtraction facts up to thirteen are optional and require six more cards. Students must find a match of two cards with play continuing until all of the matches have been made. For example, $? + 7 = 7$ is a match for $0 + ? = 7$ and $? - 0 = 7$ is a match for $7 - ? = 7$ since all the sums and all the differences equal 7. It will be helpful to explain this "matching" before any students attempt the game. The game is for 2 to 4 players.

LANGUAGE

"Is Tuesday Really Your Favorite Day?" incorporates the idea that most people have a favorite day for one reason or another. Students will keep a daily journal for two weeks, writing down the good things that happen to them on each day. They will use that record to decide which, if any, is their luckiest, and therefore, their favorite day. They will also decide which is their "not-so-lucky" day and write or dictate a sentence explaining why they think a difference exists.

A bulletin board display entitled "Some of Our Favorite Days" may feature these explanations and drawings.

Name

Date

**ACTIVITY**

# THE LUCKY(?) SEVEN

Directions: All of the words on this page have been formed from the word "Tuesday." The value of each letter is shown on the telephone buttons. Every set of 3 letters has the same number value. Look at these numbers and write them in the blanks after the letters. Then add the numbers together to get the sum to find the value of the whole word. Use a calculator. The first one is done for you. AS = A has a value of 2 and S has a value of 7. Their sum equals 9. Do all of them and you will find out what is special about every one of these words.

1. AS    A = 2  S = 7, so AS = 9
2. DAYS    D = ___ A = ___ Y = ___ S = ___, so DAYS = _____
3. EASY    E = ___ A = ___ S = ___ Y = ___, so EASY = _____
4. SAD    S = ___ A = ___ D = ___, so SAD = _____
5. SAT    S = ___ A = ___ T = ___, so SAT = _____
6. SAY    S = ___ A = ___ Y = ___, so SAY = _____
7. SEAT    S = ___ E = ___ A = ___ T = ___, so SEAT = _____
8. SET    S = ___ E = ___ T = ___, so SET = _____
9. STAY    S = ___ T = ___ A = ___ Y = ___, so STAY = _____
10. YES    Y = ___ E = ___ S = ___, so YES = _____

**The special number is _____.**

| 1 | ABC 2 | DEF 3 |
|---|---|---|
| GHI 4 | JKL 5 | MNO 6 |
| PRS 7 | TUV 8 | WXY 9 |

Name

Date

# DIRECTIONS FOR MAKING THE "HOW MANY MATCHES CAN YOU MAKE?" GAME

Copy each of the equations on 2" by 3" (5 cm by 7.5 cm) pieces of tagboard, using one color for the addition problems and a different color for the subtraction problems.

Remind the students that they must match the addition cards to addition cards and subtraction cards to subtraction cards and that all of the sums or differences on the cards are equal to 7.

| | | | | | Optional | |
|---|---|---|---|---|---|---|
| ? + 7 = 7 | ? + 5 = 7 | 4 + ? = 7 | ? – 0 = 7 | ? – 2 = 7 | | |
| 0 + ? = 7 | 2 + ? = 7 | 5 + ? = 7 | 7 – ? = 7 | 9 – ? = 7 | 11 – ? = 7 | ? – 5 = 7 |
| ? + 6 = 7 | ? + 4 = 7 | 6 + ? = 7 | ? – 1 = 7 | ? – 3 = 7 | ? – 4 = 7 | 13 – ? = 7 |
| 1 + ? = 7 | 3 + ? = 7 | 7 + ? = 7 | 8 – ? = 7 | 10 – ? = 7 | 12 – ? = 7 | ? – 6 = 7 |

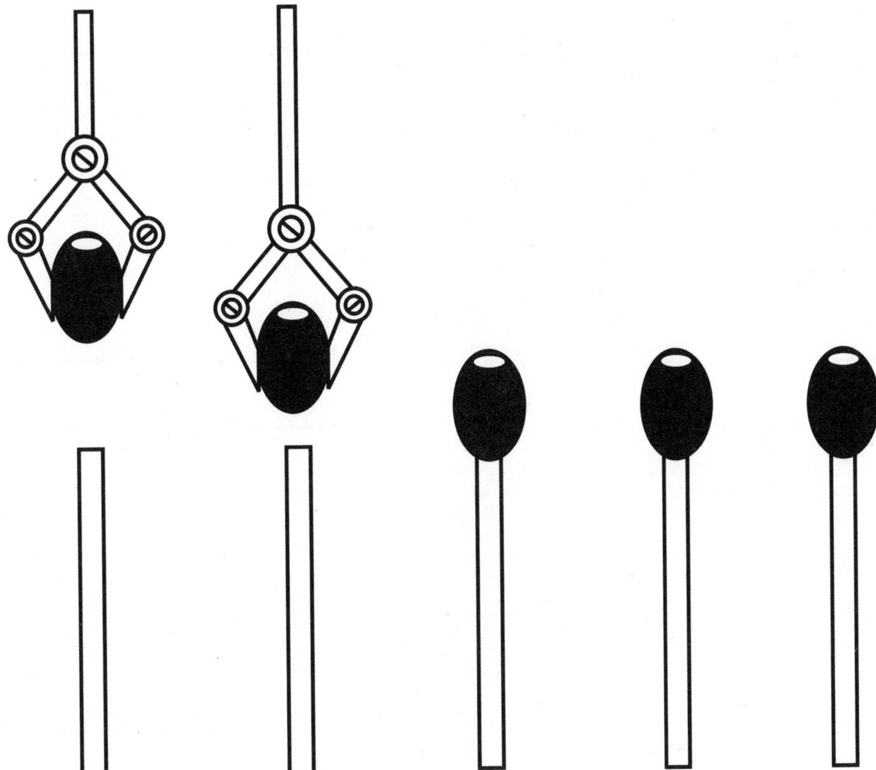

Name ______________________ Date ______________________

ACTIVITY

# HOW MANY MATCHES CAN YOU MAKE?

**Rules:**

1. This game is for 2 to 4 players.
2. A player scores when a pair of cards match. Each sum or difference equals 7.
3. Addition cards must be matched with addition cards and subtraction cards with subtraction cards. Addition and subtraction cards are shuffled separately, then placed facedown in two separate stacks on the table.
4. Each player draws three cards from either stack, then players take turns drawing one card each time.
5. If the card drawn matches one of the cards the player has he/she keeps the card and discards one of the other cards—facedown on the bottom of the deck.
6. Matching cards are placed faceup on the table in front of the players.
7. If the card drawn does not match, the player must still discard one card so that there are never more than three cards held by each player.
8. Play continues until all matches have been made, and the player with the most cards wins.
9. Copy the number sentences on your matching cards in the blanks below.

An example of an addition match is ? + 7 = 7 and 0 + ? = 7.

An example of a subtraction match is ? – 0 = 7 and 7 – ? = 7.



**Cards That Match:**

**Match 1** ______________________ ______________________

**Match 2** ______________________ ______________________

**Match 3** ______________________ ______________________

How many matches did you make? __________

Has 7 been a lucky number for you? __________

Why or why not? ______________________________________________

Name ____________________ Date ____________________

**ACTIVITY**

# IS TUESDAY REALLY YOUR FAVORITE DAY?

Directions: Use the space below to write the good things that happen to you on each day of the week for two weeks. Do more good things happen on one day than on others? Is that your favorite day?

| DAY | WEEK 1 | WEEK 2 |
| --- | --- | --- |
| Sunday | ______ | ______ |
| Monday | ______ | ______ |
| Tuesday | ______ | ______ |
| Wednesday | ______ | ______ |
| Thursday | ______ | ______ |
| Friday | ______ | ______ |
| Saturday | ______ | ______ |

Which day of the week seems to be your lucky day? What happens?

Which day of the week seems to be your not-so-lucky day? What happens?

ILLUSTRATOR:
**Peter Spier**

STANDARD:
**Problem Solving, Measurement**

CONCEPT:
**Money, Whole Numbers, Counting**

## Materials:

- "Sing a Song of Finding" activity sheet
- "Fox Counting" activity sheet
- "Why, You're as Sly as a Fox!" activity sheet
- Transparency of the words in "Sing a Song of Finding"
- Counters
- Calculators
- Dimes or other coins (optional)
- Recording of the song "The Fox Went Out on a Chilly Night" (optional)

# THE FOX WENT OUT ON A CHILLY NIGHT

A fox leaves his family to travel many miles "on a chilly night" to a farm where there are large numbers of geese and ducks just waiting to be caught. He runs quickly over the hills and across the fields until he nears the farm. Then he becomes cautious and slows down. The geese and ducks scatter and squawk and quack as the fox catches one of each and begins to run off with them. The noise wakes the farmer's wife, who looks out of the window and sees that the grey goose is gone. She wakes up her husband, who dresses in a hurry, grabs his gun, and chases the thief, stopping only long enough to blow his horn. When the fox hears that, he knows he must hurry, for the townspeople will be after him along with the farmer. He returns safely to his family, who are relieved that he has not been harmed and that he has found food for them. The fox and his wife curl up in front of their fireplace after eating a once-in-a-lifetime dinner and watch their ten little ones chewing on the bones. (The last two pages of the book feature the folk song with the words and music printed on the left-hand page, which shows the family singing while the mother plays the piano. Strangely enough, the duck and goose, both very alive, are singing with them. Verses two through seven are printed on the right-hand page with each verse headed by that number of foxes.)

## Introduction

Students need to listen to the song so they will be familiar with the melody before they become involved in the "Sing a Song of Finding" activity. Explain that the book you will be sharing with students is a folk song. Then ask the class the following to ensure that they understand just what a "folk" song is:

1. Does anyone know what a "folktale" is?
2. How can we tell if a story we hear is a folktale?
3. Has anyone ever heard of a "folk song"?
4. Does anyone know the difference between a folktale and a folk song? What is it?
5. Are there any folk songs that are listened to and sung today? What are some?

Tell them that this folk song has been illustrated for them by an artist named Peter Spier so that they can see the actions in the song as they listen to the rhymes.

Instruct students to notice the details of the beautiful illustrations so they can remember at least one of them to share in a class discussion after the story is finished. They should also listen to the song as it is sung through at least once, then sing it themselves several times in order to be familiar with the melody before proceeding to the mathematics activity "Sing a Song of Finding."

After sharing the book, ask these questions:

1. How far did the fox have to travel that night to get to the town? (many miles)
2. Where did the fox get his light? (from the moon)
3. Do you think you could find something you were hunting for at night?
4. What might you use for light instead of the moon?

Explain that they, like the fox, are going to "go out on a chilly night" to find something, and that they are going to learn a song about what they are looking for. These questions lead into the activity "Sing a Sing of Finding." This involves the class in a singing and movement exercise as well as a mathematical activity in which they will be looking for and finding dimes. Most of the students will need to use counters or real coins and/or the use of a calculator for help in doing this part of the activity. Even though the whole class has participated in the singing of the song, it will be beneficial to have them work in groups to do the calculations, or at least, to decide how they could solve the problem.



## Mathematics Activity

Students need to listen as the words of the song in the "Sing a Song of Finding" activity sheet are sung to the melody of "The Fox Went Out on a Chilly Night." This song ends with students finding a number of dimes when they go out on their own "chilly night." Once students find the dimes, each student determines how many he or she has and what that number of dimes is worth. Then students should calculate the total number of dimes found. Students then are asked to decide if they have found a large amount of money as well as how they would spend that amount of money. If the use of dimes is too difficult, substitute pennies or other counting materials with only a slight variation in the words of the song.

Once the class is familiar with the song, allow them to interpret it by moving around the room fitting their actions to the words of the song.

## Follow-Up Activities

In the "Fox Counting" activity, ask students (paired or in small groups) to look at the last double-page spread in the book. If there is a fiber-optics room available, the whole class will be able to see the pages on the overhead. This spread shows the fox family enjoying the song after they have had their meal. The activity involves counting to 10, skip counting, and counting backwards from 10.

The "Why, You're as Sly as a Fox!" activity sheet involves students in matching different characteristics of animals and insects to old familiar sayings. A word box is included to help students make the appropriate selections. This activity can be used as a type of scavenger hunt wherein each member of a small group is held responsible for finding the answers. They can take the sheet with them so that they may ask others if they know the associations. A prize or privilege should be given to the group with the most correct answers. This will be most effective when the class is organized in small groups.

Name

Date

ACTIVITY

# SING A SONG OF FINDING

Directions: Sing the words of this song to the tune of the song in the book *The Fox Went Out on a Chilly Night*. At the end of the song, count the value of the number of dimes you have found in the hunt. Then add all of the dimes together to find out how much money has been found by the whole class. You may use a calculator.

### Our Song of Hunting and Finding

Our whole class goes out on a chilly night.
With only a flashlight to give us light.
For there are many miles to go this night,
So we can find some dimes–o, dimes–o, dimes–o.
For there are many miles to go this night,
So we can find some dimes–o.

Everyone has to keep looking all around,
For there are many places money might be found.
It seems to be taking a very long time,
For us to find any dimes–o, dimes–o, dimes–o.
It seems to be taking a very long time.
For us to find some dimes–o.

We hope we are really getting near,
To where something shiny will soon appear.
Maybe this money cannot ever be found,
If only we could see some dimes–o, dimes–o, dimes–o.
Maybe this money cannot ever be found,
If only we could see some dimes–o.

What's that on the other side of the tree?
It looks very much like a dime to me.
For we have found what we came to count,
We each have found 4 dimes–o, 4 dimes–o, 4 dimes–o.
For we have found what we came to count,
We each have found our 4 dimes–o.

I found ____ dimes. Total number of dimes found by the whole class is ________.

How could you find the total value of all of the dimes?________________________________

Total value in dollars and cents ________.

Name ______________________ Date ______________________

**ACTIVITY**

# FOX COUNTING

Directions: Look at the illustrations in the book to solve the problems the fox family had. Fill in the numbers in all of the blanks.

1. How many are in the fox family? ______________________

2. Name the members of the family. ______________________

______________________

3. How many people are there in your family? ______________________

4. Are there more or less in their family than in yours? ______________________

5. Look at the picture on the very last page and count the number of foxes shown above the verse numbers listed:

   Verse 4? ________ Verse 5? ________ Verse 2? ________

   Verse 7? ________ Verse 3? ________ Verse 6? ________

6. Fill in the missing numbers of little foxes.

   1 __ __ 4 __ 6 __ __ 9 __

7. Count the number of little foxes by counting by twos.

   2 __ __ __ __

8. Count the number of little foxes by counting backwards from 10.

   10 __ __ __ __ __ __ __ __ __

9. Can you tell how many animals are in this story? How? ______________________

______________________

Name

Date

**ACTIVITY**

# WHY, YOU'RE AS SLY AS A FOX!

Directions: There are many sayings that link animals with certain traits and/or habits. Read the examples below. Then in the blank write the name of an animal that you think fits the saying best.

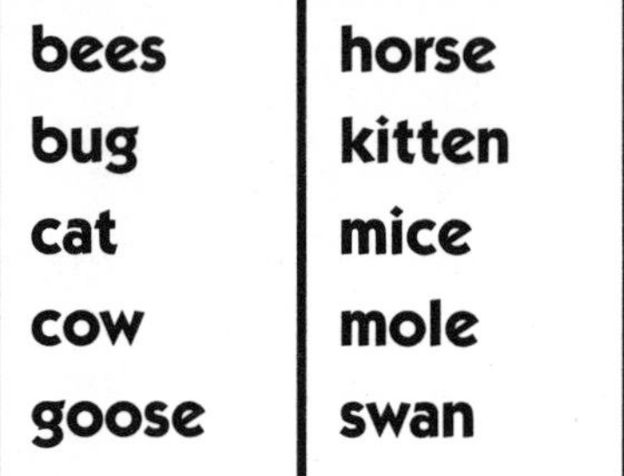

| | |
|---|---|
| **bees** | **horse** |
| **bug** | **kitten** |
| **cat** | **mice** |
| **cow** | **mole** |
| **goose** | **swan** |

1. Let's all be as busy as ______________.
2. She's as stubborn as a ______________.
3. We should all be as quiet as ______________.
4. He's as snug as a ______________ in a rug.
5. What a silly ______________ he is.
6. She's as nervous as a ______________.
7. That baby is as cute as a ______________.
8. She's as graceful as a ______________.
9. He eats like a ______________.
10. She is as contented as a ______________.

AUTHOR:

**Arnold Lobel**

STANDARD:

**Problem Solving, Geometry, Measurement of Time**

CONCEPT:

**Recognizing and Naming Shapes**



## Materials:

- Attribute shapes for each student
- Transparent attribute pieces for the overhead
- "Riddle Me One, Riddle Me Two" activity sheet
- Small desk or table dividers for each student
- "What Shape Is Your Shape In?" activity sheet
- "Changing the Calendar" activity sheet
- A calendar for each student—any year
- Calculators (optional)

# FROG AND TOAD ARE FRIENDS

This easy-to-read book contains five episodes in the lives of these good friends.

"Spring" begins as an exuberant Frog tries to awaken a sleepy Toad who has been hibernating since November. Toad refuses to wake up and get out of bed even though Frog assures him that it is warm and the sun is shining. He tells Frog to come back at half past May and goes back to bed. Frog looks at Toad's calendar and notices that the November page is still on top. He begins to tear off all of the pages of the months that have gone by while toad has slept. When he comes to April, he cannot resist tearing that page off too. He awakens Toad again, pointing to the calendar to show Toad it is May. A wide-awake Toad jumps out of bed to run outside with his friend to enjoy the lovely spring weather.

"The Story" deals with Toad's effort to think of a story to tell Frog, who is not feeling well. Toad simply cannot think of a story, no matter how hard he tries. He paces up and down on the porch, tries standing on his head, pours several glasses of water on his head, he even tries beating his head against the wall, but nothing helps. Now he is worn out, so the two exchange places and Frog tells Toad a story. Frog's story is about a toad who couldn't think of a story to tell his friend. By the time the story is finished, Toad is sound asleep.

"A Lost Button" involves the two friends in a search for a button that is missing from Toad's jacket. They retrace the places where they walked in the woods in hopes of finding it. Frog spies a black one; Toad's is white. The next button found has only two holes, not four. The next button they find is small; Toad's is large. A raccoon finds a square button, Toad's is round. Frog finds a thin button; Toad's is thick. Toad runs out of patience, runs home, and slams the door behind him. It is then that he sees his "lost" button on the floor. He collects all the buttons they found, sews them on his jacket, and gives the jacket to Frog, who loves it.

"The Swim" describes how embarrassed Toad is to be seen in his bathing suit. When he and Frog go swimming, he makes Frog promise not to look at him until after he is in the water. That's no problem. The problem comes when it is time for Toad to get out of the water and there is a turtle, some lizards, a snake, two dragonflies, and a field mouse who refuse to leave without looking at him. Poor Toad stays in the water as

**long as he can stand it, then has to get out. Sure enough, all of them—even Frog—laugh at how funny he looks.**

**"The Letter" finds Toad sitting on his porch waiting for the mailman to bring him a letter—but no one has ever written to him. When Frog finds this out, he goes home and writes a letter to his friend, gives it to a snail to deliver, then rejoins Toad on his porch. He has to confess what he has done to Toad to keep him watching for the letter. After a long time, the letter is delivered and that makes both of them very happy.**

## Introduction

Since this is an "I Can Read" book, many students will be able to read this book on their own. It is also a great book for peer reading practice and may be used for that purpose. In addition, it is the perfect book to read to the whole class when time is limited, as each story is short and complete in itself and yet each is connected through the main characters being the same in each. It serves as an excellent vehicle to elicit some discussion about the qualities and responsibilities required in a good, strong friendship. If read to the class or to a small group, use the following discussion starters:

This is a story about two great friends that you may already know, Frog and Toad, and the adventures they have together. In fact, the title is *Frog and Toad Are Friends.*

1. What do friends like to do together?
2. Is it important that both friends enjoy whatever they do? Why or why not?
3. Do friends ever try to help each other or cheer each other up? How do you help or cheer up a friend?

The activity, "Riddle Me One, Riddle Me Two" is an extension of the episode, "The Button." It can be introduced at the conclusion of that episode or at the end of the book, but an introduction to the activity should link it with the particular problem involved in trying to find the exact button that Toad lost.



## Mathematics Activity

Students should work in small groups for the "Riddle Me One, Riddle Me Two" activity. Each needs a set of attribute pieces and a small divider in front of him or her. The activity sheet requires students to remember the characteristics of the button lost by Toad and of the ones that were found. Students then choose two "buttons" from the attribute pieces and fill in the blanks describing them (or draw a picture of them), shielding their papers from the others. They then answer questions from the others about the characteristics of their "buttons" with a "yes" or "no" only until the correct identification is made. Group members must take turns asking their questions. Each member of the group must have the descriptive characteristics of their two buttons firmly in mind before the others can begin to guess which of the attribute pieces each is. The activity sheet provides a written guide for each. Groups may challenge other groups with their best "button" riddles. (Instead of using the words "thick" and "thin" to describe the buttons, "height" is used. This should be clarified for the students before they begin.)

## Follow-Up Activities

The activity, "What Shape Is Your Shape In?" has students combine the attribute pieces to make a larger designated shape or figure. As students listen to or read the names of pieces asked for in the new figure, they should place those pieces in front of them. Some students may need the help of seeing these transparent pieces on the overhead. They may work alone, in pairs, or small groups to do this activity. Once they have formed a larger shape or figure, they should trace around it to save it before going on to the next one. Some are much more complex than others. Students should be given a choice of which figures to construct. Although examples of the completed figures are shown, variations should be permitted since this is designed to be an open-ended activity. Students should take turns showing how they used the pieces to form their figures on the overhead. If plastic pieces are not available, draw the figures on the chalkboard.

# Follow-Up Activities Con't.

LANGUAGE

"Changing the Calendar" allows students to choose which months they would sleep through if they hibernated as Toad did. Any events that took place during the five months from November through March were completely lost to him. Students must decide which months they wouldn't mind losing and rearrange the calendar to adjust to fewer months by eliminating one or two months. Read sentences on the activity sheet to them one at a time. They must also decide what to do with approximately 60 days if they changed the year to ten months on the calendar but kept the same number of days. In which months would those days go—school days or vacation days? They can decide to take the months off consecutively or to skip around in their choices. Most will probably hate to miss October and December.

Calendars should be available for each child (or pair) so they may count days in various months. They may also tear off the months they wouldn't mind losing, and staple them together with a cover page explaining why they chose to eliminate those particular months.

Although the activity guides their decision making, and decisions will still be made for individual reasons, students can be paired or meet in small groups once the initial choices are made. The task then will be to see if a consensus can be reached on which month or months are the best to keep. Groups will then report their choices to other groups to determine if a choice can be agreed upon by the whole class. Make a graph to show the results.

These make an interesting bulletin board display entitled "The Mystery of the Missing Months" or place the papers in the students' portfolios.

Name ____________ Date ____________

**ACTIVITY**

# RIDDLE ME ONE, RIDDLE ME TWO

Directions: Choose two "buttons" from your attribute pieces to play a "lost button" game. Other members of your group will try to guess what your "lost buttons" look like by asking questions about them. Answer those questions only with a "yes" or a "no." First, though, think about how the buttons found were different from the button Toad lost. Follow the directions below, then see if the other members of your class can guess what your "buttons" look like. Take your turn guessing about the other buttons too! You may draw pictures of your "buttons" at the bottom of the page.

Before choosing your "buttons," fill in the blanks with the words that tell about Toad's lost button and the buttons that were found.

Toad's lost button was:

color __________ shape __________ size __________

height __________ number of holes __________

Tell how the buttons found were different from Toad's:

color __________ shape __________ size __________

height __________ number of holes __________

Choose two "buttons" from your attribute pieces. Do not let anyone else see the ones chosen. Remember which they are by filling in the blanks below.

Number 1 is a __________ color, is __________ in size, is a __________ shape, and is __________ in height.

Number 2 is a __________ color, is __________ in size, is a __________ shape, and is __________ in height.

Answer all questions asked by group members with only a "yes" or "no."

How many guesses do you think your group members will need? __________

Name

Date

# WHAT SHAPE IS YOUR SHAPE IN?

Directions: Place your attribute shapes together to form some of the larger figures described on this sheet. Trace around each figure on a sheet of paper before doing the next one. See how many of these figures you can make! Work with a partner to combine your pieces as you do numbers 4 through 7.

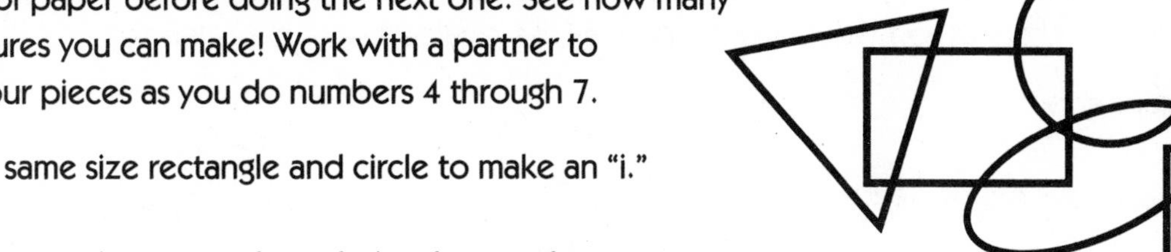

1. Use the same size rectangle and circle to make an "i."

2. Use the same size rectangle and triangle to make an arrow.

3. Use the same size rectangle and hexagon to make a sign.

4. Use a large triangle, a large circle, a small circle, and two small hexagons to make a clown head.

5. Use a large triangle, two large rectangles, two small squares, one small triangle, and one small rectangle to make a dog.

6. Use one large triangle, one large circle, one large square, two large rectangles, two small rectangles, two small circles, and two small hexagons to make a person.

7. Use a large hexagon and six small squares to make a flower.

Can you make any other figures with your pieces? Draw them here.

Name ____________ Date ____________

ACTIVITY

# CHANGING THE CALENDAR

Directions: Toad went to sleep in November and was still sleeping in March when Frog went to wake him up. Would you like to sleep that long? Do you think you would miss much? Think about what you would do if you were to sleep through some months in the year. Complete the sentences on this page to help you decide what changes you would make. You may use a calculator and a calendar.

1. Toad slept about ________ months.

   How many days did he sleep? ____________

2. Would you like to sleep that long? ________

3. Would you like to try to sleep through one month? ________ Two months? ________

   Why or why not? ____________

   ____________

4. If you slept through two months, about how many days would that be? ____________

5. Which month or months would you choose to sleep through? ____________

   Why? ____________

   ____________

6. If you decided to have just ten months a year instead of twelve but kept the same number of days in the year, where would you put those extra day? In which month or months? ____________

   ____________

7. Tell why it *is or is not* better to keep the calendar the way it is. ____________

   ____________

AUTHOR:

**Donald Hall**

STANDARD:

**Problem Solving, Measurement**

CONCEPT:

**Patterns and Relationships**



## Materials:

- "How Far Is Far?" guide sheet
- "How Far Is Far?" activity sheet
- Copy of map of Circle-o
- "Shape Up" activity sheet
- "My Contribution" activity sheet
- Rulers, markers, crayons
- A one-quarter-mile or one-quarter-kilometer walking distance
- Timer or stop watch
- Calculators

# OX-CART MAN

**On a beautiful fall day, a farmer loads his ox-cart with materials he and his family have produced throughout the year to sell at the Portsmouth Market. When the cart is fully loaded, he sets off on foot for the ten-day journey. He hopes to sell everything he has taken and he does—even the wooden box that held the maple sugar, the barrel the apples were in, the empty potato bag, the ox-cart, the ox yoke and harness, and the ox! Then he buys presents for his family—an embroidery needle from England, a Barlow knife, an iron kettle, and a bag of wintergreen peppermint candy. He also has enough money left to reinvest in the farm. His family appreciates their gifts—his son carves brooms, his daughter embroiders linens, his wife spins flax into linen, and all of them make candles. He stitches a new harness and carves a yoke for the young ox, begins building a new cart, and splits shingles. They work as a team all through the winter to prepare what they will need for the next planting season. When spring comes, they will collect and boil sap to make maple sugar. shear the sheep, spin, weave, knit, and plant their crops. The cycle of their lives follows the cycle of the seasons.**

## Introduction

Before reading the book, generate a discussion about the way people used to travel in the years before our modern transportation systems were available by asking such questions as:

1. How do you get to the movie or a sports game that is more than ten blocks away from your house? Would you want to see the movie or game badly enough to walk? How long do you think it would take you to walk ten blocks?
2. Do you usually walk to school? How far is the school from your home?
3. If you don't walk to school, how do you get here?

Explain that the story they are going to hear is about a farmer who lived a long time ago and had to walk for ten days to get where he wanted to go. After sharing the story, ask the following questions:

1. How many miles/kilometers do you think the farmer walked in the ten days?
2. Where did the farmer sleep at night? Can you tell from the story?
3. What part of the country is the setting for this story? How do you know?
4. Is there anything in this story that makes you think that it would have been nice to have lived in that time period? What?
5. Why did the farmer kiss the ox goodbye?

## Mathematics Activity

Information concerning distance walked in a certain amount of time must be established before students can be assigned the activity "How Far Is Far?" They must know how long it takes them to walk a mile or a kilometer, and, on that basis, be able to estimate how long it might take the farmer in this story to walk the same distance. A quarter mile or quarter kilometer should be marked off on the track or playground so that each student can be timed in walking that distance. Multiplying that time by four will determine how long it will take them to walk one mile or kilometer. From that information they will first estimate, then calculate, how far they think they might be able to walk in one day, in five days, and in ten days. They will use these calculations to estimate the distance both they and the farmer would travel in ten days of walking. Since his destination was Portsmouth, a general location of his farm can then be approximated by retracing his path from Portsmouth, in any direction desired, on the map provided.

Students need to work in pairs or small groups on this activity. Guidance may be needed about how they are to go about making a comparison between the time they need to walk one mile or kilometer and the time needed by an adult to walk the same distance. Ask "How could you find out how long it may take an adult to walk a mile (kilometer)?" They should come up with the idea of asking several adults if they know how long it takes them to walk a mile or a kilometer and how many hours they think they, or anyone they know, could walk in one day. Give students a set number of miles or kilometers the farmer would walk in one day.

The "How Far Is Far?" guide sheet provides extra help in making distance determinations. This activity provides an excellent opportunity for teaming with a physical education teacher on the school staff if he or she has the time to become involved. Cooperating in this activity will include an extension of the fitness component of their curriculum.

## Follow-Up Activities

Instruct students to use the "Shape Up" activity sheet as they go on a kind of scavenger hunt by looking for shapes shown in the first illustration in the book (or any other page where many shapes are included). They are to find, list, and identify as many different shapes as they can, either by writing their names or reproducing them in a drawing. When they finish, they will use many of these shapes to create a picture that represents shapes in their own home environment or that of the school, or one showing something of importance in their own lives.

The "My Contribution" activity sheet is an extension of ideas that should develop from a discussion of how thoughtful it was of the farmer to think of the needs of his family and buy gifts for them. This leads to the idea of how good it is when people work together to help each other provide for common wants and needs. Promote the thought that the class could work together to fill a want or need for the classroom that all of them can enjoy. Use the following questions as a guide in helping the students generate ideas:

1. What one thing do you think we could buy that would make it more fun to be in this classroom? How can we agree on this?
2. How much will this item cost?
3. Where can it be bought?
4. Will we need money to keep it here?
5. Where will the money to pay for it come from?
6. Could the money be earned in another way?

General limits of possibilities such as no living things, no food, nothing that is extremely noisy, and so on, should be set beforehand to forestall students coming up with impractical ideas.

Students will need a few minutes to think about and jot down individual ideas. Then ask them to work in groups of at least four in a brainstorming session. After a set time limit, each group must choose their best, most practical idea. After all ideas are shared and discussed, the class should decide on one they want to pursue.

Lists must be made of questions that need to be answered and jobs that must be done. If the problem is to be solved, various degrees of research, depending upon the choice of project, will be necessary. Each member of a group should be assigned a certain role in working toward a solution: looking through catalogs, newspaper advertisements, interviewing students in other classrooms, getting ideas from parents, thinking of ways to earn money, and so forth. Each group is responsible for a part in providing information and ideas that can be listed on the activity sheet. It may develop into a year-long project if it is worthwhile and if it may be successfully implemented.

Name ____________________ Date ____________________

# "HOW FAR IS FAR?" GUIDE SHEET

Directions: Use this worksheet as a guide in figuring the walking distances asked for in the "How Far is Far?" activity page. Fill in the information about you and the farmer to use on the map by following the directions on the "How Far Is Far?" activity sheet.

## Information About Me

It takes me __________ minutes to walk one-fourth of a mile/kilometer.

It will take me __________ to walk one mile/kilometer.

I think I can walk for __________ miles/kilometers each day.

In five days I can walk __________ miles/kilometers.

In ten days I can walk __________ miles/kilometers.

## Information About the Farmer

I think the farmer can walk __________ miles/kilometers in one day. He can walk __________ miles/kilometers in five days. He can walk __________ miles/kilometers in ten days.

| Person Walking | Days and Distance Covered | | |
|---|---|---|---|
| | Day One | Day Five | Day Ten |
| You | | | |
| Farmer | | | |

Name ______________________ Date ______________________

ACTIVITY

# HOW FAR IS FAR?

Directions: Use the map provided to answer the following questions about the farmer in *The Ox-Cart Man*. First, locate Portsmouth on the map—it is your starting place. Draw straight lines in all four directions leading away from Portsmouth each time to see in what zone the farmer and you might be after a certain number of days of walking.

1. One day North ______________ South ______________
   East ______________ West ______________
2. Five days North ______________ South ______________
   East ______________ West ______________
3. Ten days North ______________ South ______________
   East ______________ West ______________

Where do you think the farmer lives? Place an X on the map.

Now calculate where you might be after walking the same number of days.

1. One day North ______________ South ______________
   East ______________ West ______________
2. Five days North ______________ South ______________
   East ______________ West ______________
3. Ten days North ______________ South ______________
   East ______________ West ______________

Where would you like to live if you had to walk to Portsmouth for things to do or to buy? ______________

Name ______________________ Date ______________________

ACTIVITY

# MAP OF THE STATE OF CIRCLE-O

Directions: Use this map of the new state of "Circle-o" on Geometry Island to find out where you and the farmer will be after walking ten days. List the nearest town(s).

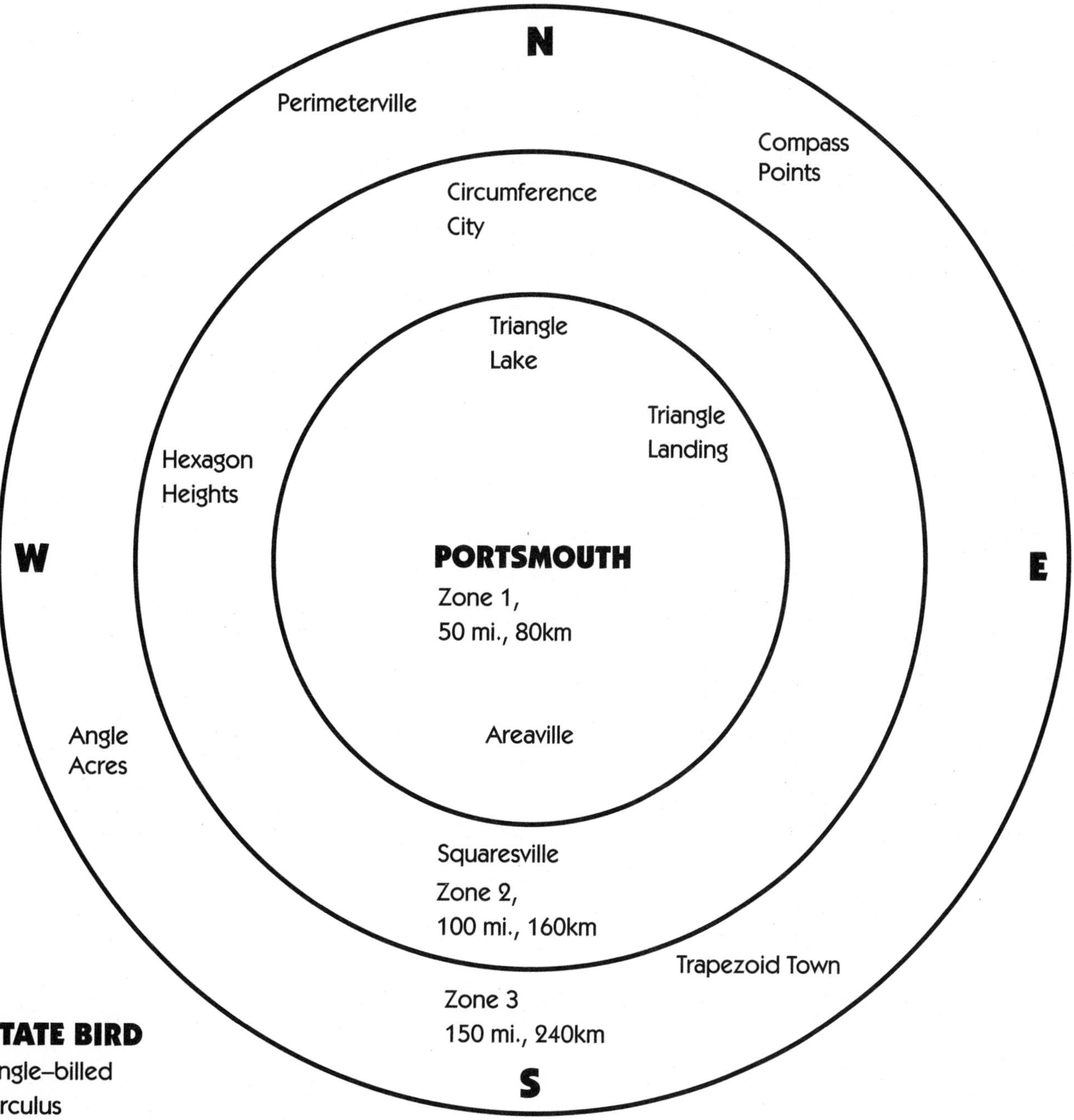

**STATE BIRD**
Angle–billed Circulus

**STATE FLOWER**
Protractor Posy

Name ______________________ Date ______________________

# SHAPE UP

Directions: Look at the first illustration in the book and write the names of all of the different shapes you see shown on that page. If you cannot remember the name of each shape, draw a picture of it on this sheet. Count the number of shapes you find and write the sum of the numbers in the space provided.

______________________ ______________________ ______________________

______________________ ______________________ ______________________

______________________ ______________________ ______________________

______________________ ______________________ ______________________

______________________ ______________________ ______________________

Total number of shapes __________

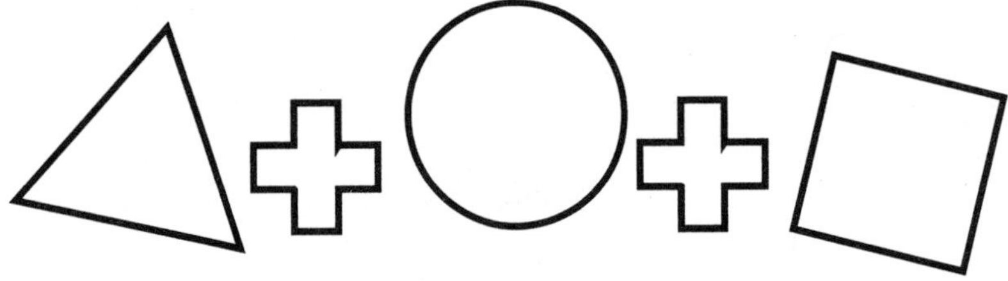

Use the space below to draw a picture, using as many of the shapes you found as you can. Draw something about your home, school, or something important in your life.

Name _______________ Date _______________

ACTIVITY

# MY CONTRIBUTION

Directions: Fill in the blanks on this page to record the information you have gathered to share with your group.

My information is about ______________________________________________

______________________________________________.

I found this by ______________________________________________

______________________________________________.

What I have found out is ______________________________________________

______________________________________________.

One important thing about this information is that ______________________________________________

______________________________________________.

This is useful because ______________________________________________

______________________________________________.

Our group can use this information to ______________________________________________

______________________________________________.

We estimate the cost of this project will be ______________________________________________

______________________________________________.

Other things to think about are ______________________________________________

______________________________________________.

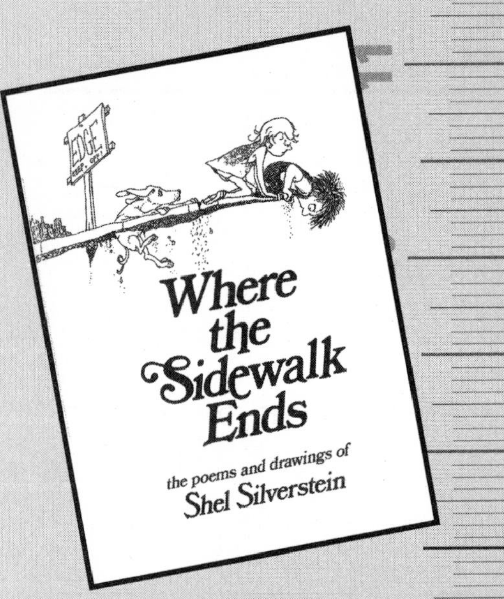


AUTHOR:

**Shel Silverstein**

STANDARD:

**Measurement, Estimation**

CONCEPT:

**Count Collections of Coins Including Pennies, Nickels, Dimes, Quarters, and Half-Dollars, and Compare Values**

## Materials:

- "Are You Money Wise?" activity sheet
- Activity sheet for creating a "Are You Money Wise?" puzzle
- "Coin Trading" activity sheet
- "Smarter!" activity sheet
- Coins or counters
- Calculators

# "SMART" FROM WHERE THE SIDEWALK ENDS

This poem clearly shows the value of one coin in relation to others and how important, in a very practical way, it is for students to be able to recognize and compare these relationships. It begins when a young boy is given a dollar by his father. The boy decides that he can show his father how very smart he is concerning the value of money. He begins by trading the one dollar for two quarters, reasoning that two is a larger amount than one. If he had stopped at that, it might not have been so bad, but he keeps right on doing his "smart" trading. He becomes more and more satisfied with himself as he keeps receiving a larger number of coins with each trade. The sad part is that he never realizes that, instead of outsmarting the others, he is the one who is being outsmarted! He consistently keeps trading down in monetary value while trading up in number of coins of lesser value. He takes great pride in receiving three dimes for two quarters and trading the four nickels for three dimes, and finally ends up exchanging the four nickels for five pennies. He rushes to tell his father of his cleverness in trading just the one-dollar bill and eventually receiving five coins in return, for he wants him to be aware of his great business sense. He is convinced his dad is proud of him when he sees his dad getting red in the face, closing his eyes, and shaking his head—and seeming quite unable to speak!

## Introduction

Discuss the following points after sharing the poem with the class:

1. Will the boy's dad really be proud of him? What do you think he will say? (Students might role-play this scene.)
2. Do you agree with what he said in the last line of each verse? Why or why not?
3. How much money did he lose in each of the individual trades?
   Trade one: two quarters for the dollar ______
   Trade two: three dimes for two quarters ______
   Trade three: four nickels for three dimes ______
   Trade four: four nickels for five pennies ______
   The total amount of money he lost is______ .
4. Explain why you think his dad will or will not ever give him a dollar again.
5. How would knowing the value of each coin have helped him?
6. How would you like to do some trading with him?

## Mathematics Activity

Distribute the "Are You Money Wise?" activity sheet and explain the rules of play to the students by doing a run–through with them using at least two examples. Modify the rules to fit the abilities of the students. In general, the only requirement is that words may be formed by moving vertically, horizontally, and/or diagonally. Explain that one letter cannot be repeated consecutively in the same word, but it can be used twice as long as a different letter has been used in between. One cannot jump over one letter to get to another one.

Point out that students should decide whether to spend the most time trying to find longer words that are worth more or to begin by finding as many two- and three-letter words as they can. They must estimate which tactic will increase their score most quickly. Place a time limit on the activity to eliminate any frustration of those students having difficulty in finding words. Students may work alone, in pairs, or small groups. You can also place this in an activity center or workstation for an ongoing challenge.

At the conclusion of the allotted playing time, students must be given additional time to total the monetary value of his or her list, or that of the group. They can use calculators to check the accuracy of each score. They can share words having the most monetary value with the class, either orally or by posting on a bulletin board for the class to explore and to improve vocabulary and authenticate the value of the lists.

Create activity sheets for a specific class based on the vocabulary being studied in the curriculum by using the model provided.

A model of the activity sheet is provided for the use of those advanced students who may wish to create and assign different values for words of a certain number of letters.

## Follow-Up Activities

The "Coin Trading" activity sheet will help students focus on the many "smart" ways to exchange coins for a dollar. They will need to determine the number of ways to combine pennies, nickels, dimes, quarters, and half-dollars to equal one dollar. This may be used as a group or individual activity. The task is to find:

1. The smallest number of these coins that are equal to one dollar.
2. The largest number of coins equal to one dollar.
3. Two ways of using some of each of the coins to equal one dollar.

Have children compare solutions within groups and/or in a whole-class activity.

Reread the poem and use it as a model for students in writing their own poem or short story about money. The "Smarter" activity sheet serves as a guide for the writing which may be a cooperative venture. Read the poem or story after introducing the idea of not being a smart trader or use it to show what really smart trades could be made.

An alternate writing assignment is to have students write a short story about what happens after the boy's father calms down and talks to him about the value of money. This could include advice from the students to the boy on how he might make better trades the next time if he gets the chance. This is also a delightful poem to dramatize with students adding their own original dialogue.

Name ____________ Date ____________

ACTIVITY

# ARE YOU MONEY WISE?

Directions: Study the letters in the chart and write as many words as you can in the time allowed. Each word you form will be worth a certain amount of money:

Two letter words are worth 2 cents

Three letter words are worth 4 cents

Four letter words are worth 6 cents

Five letter words are worth 8 cents

Any longer words are worth 12 cents each

Before starting, decide how you should "spend" your time on this puzzle—should you search for the longer, higher money value words first which may take longer to find or try to find all of the shorter, lower value money words first that you may find more quickly?

Rules: Move in any direction to form a word, but do not lift your pencil to jump over one letter to get to another one. Use the same letter twice only if there is another letter in between the two.

When time is called, add the money value of each of your words, then find the total worth of your words in money. Check your addition by using a calculator.

| C | A | S | H |
|---|---|---|---|
| C | A | R | L |
| O | I | T | E |
| P | S | N | D |

Name ______________________

Date ______________________

# MY OWN "MONEY WISE" PUZZLE

Directions: Look at the letters in the boxes and find as many words as you can using these letters. Each word is worth a certain amount of money. For example:

Two-letter words are worth ______ cents.

Three-letter words are worth _____ cents.

Four-letter words are worth ______ cents.

Five-letter words are worth _______ cents.

Longer words are worth _________ cents.

When you are done, add the total value of each word. Then add the total value of all of your words.

| C | A | S | H |
|---|---|---|---|
| | | | |
| | | | |
| | | | |

Name

**ACTIVITY**

Date

# COIN TRADING

Directions: Think about the many ways there are to combine pennies, nickels, dimes, quarters, and half-dollars to equal a one-dollar bill. Work with coins or counters and write your answers in the table below. List any other ways you can think of to combine coins to equal a dollar in the space below the table.

Find three things:

1. The smallest number of coins equal to one dollar.

2. The largest number of coins to equal one dollar.

3. Two ways of using some of each of the coins mentioned to equal one dollar.

Compare your table with that of your classmates when you have finished filling in the table.
Use this table.

| **Pennies** | **Nickels** | **Dimes** | **Quarters** | **Half-Dollars** |
|---|---|---|---|---|
| | | | | |
| | | | | |
| | | | | |
| | | | | |
| | | | | |
| | | | | |

Name

Date

# SMARTER!

Directions: This is your chance to write a poem or a short story about trading things. Try to be a lot smarter than the boy in Shel Silverstein's poem and wind up with a trade that will make everyone very PROUD of you! Use this guide if you wish. Then complete the poem or story in any way and/or form you like.

I had some good luck one day when I put a quarter in the gum machine and a whole row of coins fell out of the coin return slot. I was just starting to count them when my brother's friend came along and said he had something he would trade for that row of coins.

So I said ______________ and traded the coins for his ______________

because ______________.

After that I met ______________ who offered me ______________.

In that trade I ______________.

That might have been enough, then I met ______________.

Who was willing to give me ______________.

I couldn't refuse such a great offer so I ______________.

I might have made other trades just as "smart" but right then my little sister came riding by on her bicycle and told me it was time to go home . . . and I did.

When I told my family all about my trades, I could see how proud they were of me by the way

each of them ______________.

AUTHOR:

**Ann Grifalconi**

STANDARD:

**Describe, Draw, and Classify Shapes**

CONCEPT:

**Create Shapes with Tiles and Pattern Blocks, Use Mathematically Correct Names for Shapes**

## Materials:

- "When Are You Coming 'Round?" activity sheet
- "The Best House" activity sheet
- "Do You Remember. . . ?" activity sheet
- "Back to Square One" activity sheet
- Pattern block pieces, color tiles, or tangrams
- Geoboards and rubber bands
- Graph paper, geometric dot paper
- Markers, crayons, or pencils

# THE VILLAGE OF ROUND AND SQUARE HOUSES

This story is told by a young girl who has grown up in a village in which the men all live together in square houses and the women all live together in round houses. After the day's work is completed, the men join the women and children in the round houses to eat supper. The men always eat first, then the women, and then the children. After everyone has eaten, the men return to their square houses to smoke their pipes and talk, and the women visit among themselves in the round houses. There are reasons for why these people live in these houses and have these jobs. Long ago, the volcanic mountain Naka erupted in the middle of the night and into the next morning, and the villagers had to flee for their lives. When Naka quieted down, the villagers were unrecognizable, for they were covered with gray ashes. When they returned to the village, they saw that there were only two houses left, a square house and a round house. The chief, deciding they must rebuild at once, instructed the tall gray shapes to live in the square houses and the round gray ones to live in the round houses. The small gray ones were given the task of clearing stones from the fields. That is why women still live in round houses and cook the meals, men live in square houses and work in the fields, and children keep the fields free of stones. The girl's grandmother says that the village remains peaceful because people know that there is a time to be apart and a time to be together, and that they will continue to live in this way as long as Naka allows them to do so!

## Introduction

Introduce this book by asking if anyone can describe the shape of the house in which he or she lives. After listening to and discussing various responses, ask if anyone has ever seen a round house and what it might be like to live in one. This is a natural lead-in to show the cover of the book and explain that they are going to listen to a story about people who live in two differently shaped houses. Be sure to read the author's note on the back of the title page. After sharing the story, use the following questions to elicit discussion and comprehension:

1. Would it be fun to live in a round house? Why or why not?

2. What problems can you think of that would be caused by living in a house with no corners?
3. What do you suppose the girl from the village thought when she first saw that other people did not live in houses made of just two different shapes?
4. What happens when a volcano erupts?
5. Can you name any famous volcanic eruptions?
6. How many different shapes do you see in this classroom?
7. Look at your pattern block pieces, tiles, and tangrams. Can you name each shape?
8. How many of these shapes could be used in the building of a house?

## Mathematics Activity

This activity consists of matching the names of different shapes to nonstandard but everyday definitions by filling in the names in the blanks on the "When Are You Coming 'Round?" activity sheet. The correct spellings of the names are shown in the word box. Students read the names of the shapes, then the definitions, and then choose a shape that fits each definition and copy it onto the blank. Tell students that they may have to stretch their imaginations for some of the definitions. If you read the activity sheet to them, read sentences one by one, allowing students enough time to complete each before going on. After students fill in all of the blanks, they should write the marked letters in the blanks at the bottom of the page to give the answer, which is "To eat a meal." The use of cooperative learning groups is excellent for this activity but students may work in other ways if desired. If working in groups, pairs should share and then compare with other pairs in the group to reach agreement as to the connection between the geometric figure and the name.



## Follow-Up Activities

Students will use any combination of pattern block shapes, tiles, or tangrams to form as many differently shaped houses as they can in the activity "Back to Square One?" The outline of each shape should be traced and given to another student or be duplicated and placed in an activity center to challenge classmates to arrange the pieces in the same pattern. One of the pieces of the design could be omitted as an additional challenge. The number and kind of shape used must be stated (2 hexagons, 1 triangle, 1 mystery shape). Students may also try to create the design using fewer or more shapes than there are in the original one. A variation of this activity may be done using geoboards, rubber bands, and dot paper to create house shapes and record each shape on the dot paper. Hold a contest to see which student can create the most shapes.

Using the activity sheet, "The Best House," students write a story and draw a picture of "The Best House" to show how they would look and feel living in such a house.

An alternative assignment is to have students use the activity sheet "Do You Remember. . . ?" to interview a family member—parent, grandparent, any older relative or adult—about the custom(s) they have in their own families, or even in their towns, and their origins. The interview should be recorded on an audio- or videotape. Students can present an oral report on the customs for a small group or the whole class or write a short story about them.

Students should share stories and make comparisons after posting them on a bulletin board entitled, "Our Customs."

Name ____________________  Date ____________________

**ACTIVITY**

# WHEN ARE YOU COMING 'ROUND?

Directions: Read the names of the shapes in the box and then read the sentences that define them. Choose the shape the sentence describes, and copy it in the blank. (Remember: You will not fill in all of the blanks.)

| | | | | |
|---|---|---|---|---|
| **Circle** | **Rhombus** | **Square** | **Cube** | **Hexagon** |
| **Cylinder** | **Sphere** | **Trapezoid** | **Rectangle** | **Triangle** |

1. My name sounds like something a hunter would do. (_) _ _ _ _ _ _ _ _ _
2. Bees feel right at home with my shape. _ _ _ _ _ (_) _ _ _
3. Sometimes I'm very cold, and sometimes I'm decorated with dots. _ _ _ (_) _ _ _ _ _
4. You may see me right in the center of a town. _ _ _ (_) _ _ _ _ _
5. Something you wear on your feet may come in a box of my shape. _ _ _ (_) _ _ _ _ _
6. Some people call me a diamond but that is not my real name. _ _ _ (_) _ _ _ _ _
7. I never play the angles and I'm never cornered. _ _ _ _ _ (_) _ _ _
8. Sometimes I am right, sometimes I am not. _ _ _ (_) _ _ _ _ _
9. A lot of different kinds of canned foods are packaged in my shape. _ _ (_) _ _ _ _ _ _ _
10. My shape is very important to people who play baseball. (_) _ _ _ _ _

Copy the marked letters in the blanks below. If you have identified each shape correctly, you will have the answer to the question, "When Are You Coming 'Round?" that fits the custom in the story of the round and square houses. _ _   _ _ _ _   _ _ _ _ _ _

Name

Date

# BACK TO SQUARE ONE?

Directions: Use your pattern block shapes, your tiles, or your tangrams (or all of them) to form at least two different kinds of houses. Trace the outline of each shape on this page before doing another one. Include the names of the pieces used but do not draw their outlines. Trade papers with a classmate to see if each of you can copy the pattern the other made.

Name ______________________

Date ______________________

# THE BEST HOUSE

Directions: Write a story about living in a round or square house by completing the sentences below. The space at the bottom of the page is for you to draw a picture of this "Best House," or a picture of how you would look and feel living in "The Best House."

The shape of the house I live in is ____________, and I think it is really ______________________.

When we first moved into it, I thought, "Gee, this is going to be ______________________

______________________________________________."

What I said about the house was ______________________

______________________________________________.

Because we live in this shape of a house, we have to eat food shaped like ____________ and have furniture that is ____________.

If I had the choice of living in any shaped house I would choose ______________________

because ______________________________________________.

Name _______________ Date _______________

**ACTIVITY**

# DO YOU REMEMBER. . . ?

Directions: Talk to a relative or other adult to find out what customs or celebrations there are in their—or your—family. Try asking some of the following questions.

1. What did you do to celebrate your birthday when you were my age? _______________

_______________

2. Was there a special way you celebrated Thanksgiving? Where did you go? Were there special foods that you always had? What were they? _______________

_______________

3. What other holidays did you observe? What did you do that was special or different? _______________

_______________

4. Was there a special place you always went for a vacation? Where? _______________

_______________

5. What was the best family custom that you remember? _______________

_______________

6. What was the best time you have ever had with your family? _______________

_______________

AUTHOR:
**Verna Aardema**

STANDARD:
**Patterns and Relationships, Problem Solving**

CONCEPT:
**Identifying Patterns, Number Recognition**

## Materials:

- "Stop Bugging Me!" activity sheet
- "Let Me Count the Ways" activity sheet
- "How About Some Scrambled Letters for Breakfast?" activity sheet
- Pictures of insects that sting or bite—mosquitoes, honeybees, giant water bugs, and fleas
- Poem "Mosquitoes, Mosquitoes!" in *Something Big Has Been Here* by Jack Prelutsky
- *Let's Find out about Mosquitoes* by David Webster
- *Insects All Around Us* by Richard Armour

# WHY MOSQUITOES BUZZ IN PEOPLE'S EARS

This *pourquoi* story is beautifully illustrated by Leo and Diane Dillon and explains why the mosquito, to this very day, is still so annoying to all of us.

An impatient iguana becomes disgusted with the mosquito who interrupts him to tell him a lie. He refuses to listen and succeeds in blocking her out by putting a stick in each ear. Now he cannot hear anything. He leaves the mosquito and goes on his way through the forest. When he doesn't respond to the python's friendly "good morning" greeting, the python is alarmed, and so, in turn, are the rabbit, the crow, and the monkey. This causes a disaster. The monkey, in his haste to warn the other animals of the forest that danger is near, accidentally causes the death of an owlet. When Mother Owl returns to her nest and finds that one of her owlets is dead, she is so distraught that she fails to carry out her duty of awakening the sun. King Lion summons Mother Owl to find out why she is allowing the night to last so long. She tells him she is too sad to awaken the sun since Monkey killed her owlet. One by one, the others are sent for and each one blames the next one for causing the owlet's death. The iguana, who still has the sticks in his ears, is unaware of what has happened until he is sent for. He explains that the mosquito is the one who started it all because of her lie. It is agreed that the mosquito is the one to be punished, but she remains hidden. Because of her guilty conscience, though, she still keeps buzzing in people's ears, asking if everyone is angry with her. She gets the answer soon enough!

## Introduction

Ask the following questions before reading the story:

1. How many of you like mosquitoes?
2. Has anyone ever been bitten by a mosquito?
3. Do you ever know when a mosquito is around? How?
4. What sound does a mosquito make? Can you imitate it?
5. Why do mosquitoes sting people?

Explain that the story they are about to hear will tell them just why a mosquito does sting people, and why it can be such a nuisance. Share the story twice with the class, the second time just before assigning the activity sheet "Let Me Count the Ways."

## Mathematics Activity

Have students make comparisons about the variations in size and characteristics of mosquitoes, honeybees, fleas, and giant water bugs, all of which have a stinger and/or will bite people. The "Stop Bugging Me!" activity sheet offers students a chance to test their knowledge of these different, yet similar, insects. If possible, make two books, *Let's Find out about Mosquitoes* and *Insects All Around Us,* available as reference sources for this activity.

## Follow-Up Activities

The "Let Me Count the Ways" activity sheet focuses on the patterns of the questions and responses of the animals when interviewed by King Lion. It may also be used as a guide sheet for a dramatization of the story. This story provides an excellent opportunity to involve everyone in the class in a re-creation of the action. Additional animal roles (as "extras") may be assigned beyond the direct speaking parts in the story.

Discuss the poem, "Mosquitoes, Mosquitoes!" then distribute the activity sheet, "How About Some Scrambled Letters for Breakfast?" Tell the students that the animals became so upset and worried when Mother Owl did not awaken the sun that somehow their names became all scrambled together and now they cannot unscramble them. If needed, review the name of each animal.

Name ____________________ Date ____________________

ACTIVITY

# STOP BUGGING ME!

Directions: Choose a name from those listed to complete each sentence that states a fact about bees, fleas, mosquitoes, and giant water bugs. If you're not sure, just think about what you know about each and make a good guess. Then check your score with the Answer Key. To find out more about each one, read *Let's Find Out About Mosquitoes* by David Webster and *Insects All Around Us* by Richard Armour.

**BEE(S)** **FLEA(S)** **MOSQUITO(ES)** **GIANT WATER BUG(S)**

1. Only female __________ bite.
2. The __________ kills its prey first, then sucks its blood.
3. The life span of a __________ is from one month to six weeks.
4. A __________ can jump a distance of 13 inches/33.02 centimeters.
5. If you race your bicycle with a __________, it will win because it can fly at the rate of 30 miles/ 48 kilometers per hour.
6. The __________ can fly fast enough to catch birds.
7. A female __________ is so light, she can walk on the surface of the water.
8. A __________ grows no longer than one-tenth of an inch/0.254 centimeters.
9. The bodies of __________ contain three parts.
10. A __________ dies after it stings just one person.

My score is __________.

A score of 8 shows you have a high I.Q. (Insect Quotient).

A score of 5 shows you know how to avoid being stung or bitten.

A lower score shows you don't do much buzzing around with bugs.

Name ____________________ Date ____________________

**ACTIVITY**

# LET ME COUNT THE WAYS

Directions: King Lion called a meeting of the animals to find out why Mother Owl had not awakened the sun. He used a two-way pattern for finding out who was responsible for this. Fill in the names of the animals in both patterns. Names are listed in the box at the bottom of the page if you need help. Each name is used twice.

| King Lion Calls the | Who Says the Trouble-Maker is |
|---|---|
| 1. ____________________ | ____________________ |
| 2. ____________________ | ____________________ |
| 3. ____________________ | ____________________ |
| 4. ____________________ | ____________________ |
| 5. ____________________ | ____________________ |
| 6. ____________________ | ____________________ |

King Lion tells the council that the one who really caused the trouble is the __________ because she annoyed the __________ who then scared the __________ who, in turn, scared the __________. She frightened the __________ who startled the __________, who killed the __________.

This was the reason that the __________ didn't awaken the sun. Unfortunately, the __________ was never found and punished!

| | | |
|---|---|---|
| **Crow**<br>**Iguana**<br>**Monkey** | **Mosquito**<br>**Mother Owl** | **Owlet**<br>**Python**<br>**Rabbit** |

Name ____________ Date ____________

ACTIVITY

# HOW ABOUT SOME SCRAMBLED LETTERS FOR BREAKFAST?

Directions: The animals in this story became so upset when the sun didn't appear that the letters in their names became all scrambled and no one knows who he or she is anymore. Help them to get back the right spellings so they can go about their business in the forest. Write the correct name in the blank opposite the scrambled name.

1. YOKMEN ____________
2. AAUGIN ____________
3. TOWEL ____________
4. EKASN ____________
5. WROC ____________
6. GKNI NILO ____________
7. BIBART ____________
8. SMOTUIOQ ____________



Explain who you think was really the guilty party in this story—who actually caused the death of the owlet? Then draw a picture of the guilty one in the space below.

AUTHOR:
**Sorche Nic Leodhas**

STANDARD:
**Estimation and Mental Computation**

CONCEPT:
**Whole Numbers, Measurement**

## Materials:

- "Will the Walls Come Tumbling Down?" activity sheet
- "Daffy Definitions" activity sheet
- "No Room for Any More" game rules
- Directions for making the game cards and game board for "No Room for Any More"
- 10" by 16" (25 cm by 40 cm) piece of blue tagboard for the game board or a large file folder
- 12 pieces of 2" by 3" (5 cm by 7.5 cm) yellow tagboard for addition problem cards
- 12 pieces of 2" by 3" (5 cm by 7.5 cm) blue tagboard for subtraction problem cards
- 12 pieces of 2" by 3" (5 cm by 7.5 cm) green tagboard for the answer cards (optional for game variation)
- 12 pieces of 2" by 3" (5 cm by 7.5 cm) white tagboard for subtraction answer cards (optional for game variation)
- Calculators
- 4 game tokens and a die
- Yardstick or meter stick (optional)
- Masking tape (optional)



# ALWAYS ROOM FOR ONE MORE

**This story describes what happens when Lachie Mac Lachan, who is always willing to share his hospitality with others, is almost too generous for his own good. When he sees that a storm is approaching, he calls to travelers to take shelter in his small hut, assuring them that there is "always room for one more"! A variety of travelers, needing shelter, soon fill the hut. The house bulges with people but Lachie insists there is still "room for one more." The house splits apart almost before the words are out of his mouth. All of his visitors, Lachie, his wife, and their ten children, are thrown outside where they stare in disbelief at what remains of the house. The travelers gather themselves up and decide they must rebuild the house to repay Lachie for his kindness. The new house is a great roomy one large enough to hold an army in the event one would come marching by. In addition, there is room for anyone and everyone else who might show up needing a place to stay. Lachie and his family are happy to know that now they do have a house that will always hold at least "one more."**

## Introduction

Ask the following questions prior to sharing this story. They focus attention on the variations in the way people speak and the words that are used in different parts of the world.

1. Do you ever hear your grandparents, parents, or other adults talk using different kinds of expressions or words from those of you and your friends?
2. Why do you think this happens?
3. Some books of historical fiction use words that we no longer hear in everyday conversation. Why do you think this happens?
4. What is a good way to find the meaning of some of words you do not use?

Inform the students that they are going to hear a story in which Scottish characters speak in a very distinctive and sometimes different way from what they are used to hearing.

Before reading the book, ask students to raise their hands, as you read the story, if they hear any unfamiliar words. After the reading, write these words on the chalkboard or overhead transparency. Arrange the class in groups and give each group one of the words that needs defining, asking the groups to try to deduce the meaning from the context of the story. If desired, all groups may work with all of the words, then compare their definitions. This may also be used for the "Daffy Definitions" activity.

## Mathematics Activity

The game "No Room for Any More" provides students with practice in solving addition and subtraction problems. Some students will need calculators to find the solutions. One student shuffles the cards and then places them facedown in the middle of the playing surface. Players take turns rolling a die and drawing a card. If they give the correct answer, they move the number of spaces indicated on the die. If not, they stay where they are. They will follow the path of footprints around the game board. Students place discards facedown on the bottom of the deck. The player who reaches the finish line first is the one who knows that the house is about to fall down and calls out, "No Room for Any More!" to end the game.

A variation of the game may also be played in "Concentration" fashion by adding answer cards. Addition and subtraction cards are kept separate. Question and answer cards either in the addition or subtraction category are placed facedown, then players take turns turning up one of each kind to see if the cards match. If they do, the player collects them. If there is no match, both cards are placed facedown again. Play ends when all of the cards have been matched or if a time limit you've set is met. The player with the most matches wins the game.

## Follow-Up Activities

"Will the Walls Come Tumbling Down?" involves students in a problem-solving exercise to determine how many students will fit in their classroom. Students go to an assigned wall and stand side by side along the wall to determine how many of them are needed to equal the length of a wall. If there are not enough students to reach along the entire distance, place a piece of masking tape where the last student is standing (or the last student in the line could remain there). The line can re-form until the length of the wall has been measured, and number of students who fit along one specified wall is counted and recorded. Organize the class into four groups with each group being responsible for measuring along one wall. They will then need to add the total number along each wall to know how many are needed to keep the walls from falling in. Ask students to decide if standing in a line instead of shoulder to shoulder would make a difference in the numbers. This information is used to enable them to estimate how many students would fill the classroom. They must then devise a plan on verifying this number.

The "Daffy Definitions" activity gives students a chance to interpret definitions given for two descriptive rhyming words. A word box is included with rhyming suggestions. Students should be organized in groups and a contest may be held to see which definitions sound the best. For example:

| **Definition** | **Word Rhymes** |
|---|---|
| 1. How your feet look in new shoes. | Neat feet. |
| 2. The last explosion. | Last blast. |

Name

Date

ACTIVITY

# RULES FOR PLAYING THE "NO ROOM FOR ANY MORE" GAME

## Game One Rules

The game is for 2 to 4 players. A die is needed.

Each player chooses a token. Shuffle the cards and place them facedown in the middle of the table.

Each player rolls the die to determine who goes first. The lowest number goes first, then play moves to the right around the table.

Each player draws a problem card. After giving the right answer, the player moves ahead the number of spaces rolled on the die. If the player does not give the right answer, he or she does not move. Each card is then placed facedown on the bottom of the deck. (Calculators may be used.) Whoever reaches the finish line first knows that the house is about to fall down and calls out, "No Room for Any More," winning the game.

## Game Two Rules

This game is played just like "Concentration," so individuals or pairs may play. The object of the game is to find a card with a sum or difference that is the solution to the question card—a match. Students place either addition problem and answer cards or subtraction problem and answer cards facedown in single rows on the table. Addition and subtraction cards are kept separate. Students turn over one problem card and one answer card. If the problem and answer fit together, the player has made a match and keeps the cards. If not, he or she turns both cards facedown again and play continues. The game ends when all of the matches have been made. If more than one player plays, the winner is the one with the most cards at the end of the game.

Name ______________________ Date ______________________

**ACTIVITY**

# DIRECTIONS FOR MAKING THE "NO ROOM FOR ANY MORE" GAME

## Game Cards

Copy the following problems on 2" by 3" (5 cm by 7.5 cm) tagboard cards—one color for addition card problems, another for subtraction card problems. Problems may be varied to suit the needs and abilities of the class. For game version 1, do not copy the answers. For game version 2, copy the answers.

| 1. | 2. | 3. | 4. | 5. | 6. |
|---|---|---|---|---|---|
| 15 | 20 | 59 | 48 | 65 | 37 |
| +50 | +49 | +21 | +36 | +27 | +34 |
| 65 | 69 | 80 | 84 | 92 | 71 |

| 7. | 8. | 9. | 10. | 11. | 12. |
|---|---|---|---|---|---|
| 26 | 14 | 52 | 17 | 23 | 45 |
| +32 | +13 | +19 | +33 | +49 | +45 |
| 58 | 27 | 71 | 50 | 72 | 90 |

| 13. | 14. | 15. | 16. | 17. | 18. |
|---|---|---|---|---|---|
| 79 | 68 | 43 | 72 | 59 | 46 |
| -39 | -66 | -28 | -45 | -21 | -19 |
| 40 | 2 | 15 | 27 | 38 | 27 |

| 19. | 20. | 21. | 22. | 23. | 24. |
|---|---|---|---|---|---|
| 38 | 22 | 99 | 62 | 66 | 22 |
| -9 | -10 | -90 | -29 | -16 | -9 |
| 29 | 12 | 9 | 33 | 50 | 13 |

## Game Board

Print the following on random spaces on the game board: Go back 2 spaces—too many people in here," "Move ahead 3 spaces—there is still plenty of room," "Party begins—move ahead 2 spaces," and "Start over—the house fell down." Enlarge the game board pattern below and either draw or glue it onto a file folder or a piece of 10" by 16" (25 cm by 40 cm) blue posterboard.

**FINISH**

**START**

Name ____________________ Date ____________________

ACTIVITY

# WILL THE WALLS COME TUMBLING DOWN?

Directions: Estimate how many of your group it will take to fill the length of your assigned wall and write it down. Move to the wall and line up shoulder to shoulder. If there are not enough of you to reach the end of the wall, leave the last person standing in place and start the line over again from that person. Be sure to keep track of how many of you it took to keep the wall from tumbling down.

## Estimate

1. Number of students in our group ____________.
2. Number it will take to line the entire wall standing shoulder to shoulder ____________.

## Actual Line

3. It took ____________ of us to fill the length of the wall.
4. Numbers needed by the other groups: ____________ ____________ ____________
5. The total number of students needed to keep the classroom walls from falling down is ____________.
6. What might be the reason for any difference in the number of students needed to fill the various walls? ______________________________________________________________.
7. How many students do you think it would take to fill your entire classroom until there was no longer any room for even one more? How could you find this number? ______________________________________________________________.
8. Would it make a difference if you measured the wall standing in a line instead of beside each other? Why or why not? ______________________________________________________________.

Name _______________ Date _______________

ACTIVITY

# DAFFY DEFINITIONS

Directions: Rewrite the definitions below as two rhyming words that you see in the word box. Work with a partner or in a group to find the rhymes that fit best.



1. Someone who steals a book. ____________ ____________
2. A ten-dollar bill that makes you laugh. ____________ ____________
3. A really good dessert. ____________ ____________
4. Fun on the ice. ____________ ____________
5. A wonderful cow. ____________ ____________
6. The school cafeteria. ____________ ____________
7. A long distance beside the ocean. ____________ ____________
8. A horse from Norway. ____________ ____________
9. A bear who likes a challenge. ____________ ____________
10. A cat with a baseball job. ____________ ____________
11. A steer that stands close to you. ____________ ____________
12. When play time is over. ____________ ____________

| | | |
|---|---|---|
| **Bat Cat** | **Funny Money** | **Noon Room** |
| **Book Crook** | **Great Skate** | **Norse Horse** |
| **Dare Bear** | **More Shore** | **Sweet Treat** |
| **Fun Done** | **Near Steer** | **Wow Cow** |

AUTHOR:
**Eric Rohmann**

STANDARD:
**Problem Solving**

CONCEPT:
**Measurement of Time**

## Materials:

- "How Can You Make Time Stand Still?" activity sheet
- "Time Savers" activity sheet
- "I Saw a ______________" activity sheet
- Poem "I Saw a Brontosaurus" in Jack Prelutsky's *Something Big Has Been Here*

# TIME FLIES

A very small bird swoops through the treetops and flies into an open window of a museum that houses an exhibit of dinosaurs. It seems fascinated by what it sees. The small size of the bird sharply contrasts with the huge sizes of the dinosaurs, which, according to theory, are the ancestors of birds. The bird continues to explore the museum, thereby beginning a descent into the past. Little by little, skin begins to cover the skeletons of the dinosaurs, which makes them look even more dangerous and threatening. The bird has to soar high in the sky to avoid one that is pursuing it as they come to life. Another dinosaur, more menacing, advances with its mouth wide open and swallows the bird whole. As the bird hovers just above the tongue of its captor a way opens for its escape, for the skin of the dinosaur begins to disappear and the skeleton shows again. The bird flies to freedom and leaves the museum, apparently having had enough of this dangerous kind of exploring. It turns its back on the past and flies far away from the ancient time to return to the safety of the present.

## Introduction

Before sharing the book, ask the following questions:

1. Is there anyone in this class who knows a lot about dinosaurs? What is one thing that you can tell us about them?
2. How many of you can name a dinosaur when you see a picture of one?
3. How long ago did the dinosaurs live?
4. Does anyone know a reason why there are no dinosaurs anymore?
5. Has anyone ever heard that dinosaurs are the ancestors of birds? What do you think about that?

Explain that this book has no words but that they can tell the story from the pictures. Then share the book.

## Mathematics Activity

The "How Can You Make Time Stand Still?" activity sheet consists of a series of sayings about time. The word box contains the missing words in each saying, and there are more words than can be used. The marked letters are written in the blanks at the bottom of the page to give the answer to the title of the activity sheet. Use this to examine the concepts of time that students have acquired. Some classes may need a little advance preparation for this exercise. A quick review of what is known about time may help.

## Follow-Up Activities

The activity sheet "Time Savers" involves the students in thinking about the ways in which they spend their time and how they can save time. Once they list these amounts of time saved, students must explain how they will use the time which they have planned to save.

An alternate activity is for students to construct a time line of the important events in their own lives, or, if this is to be a whole-class activity, it may be a time line of the events experienced by the class from the beginning of the year, such as various holiday events, or birthday celebrations, winning a school award, etc.

Read the Jack Prelutsky poem, "I Saw a Brontosaurus" in his book *Something Big Has Been Here,* to the whole-class. Students can then fill in the blanks on the activity sheet, "I Saw a ____________________." The sheets may be shared in small and/or large groups, or posted on a bulletin board entitled "What We Saw!!!" to be read by the whole class.

An alternate activity is for students to dramatize the action of *Time Flies*. Small groups of students should spend time examining the illustrations in the book so that they can invent dialogue to bring the story to life. One student (or two) will assume the role of the bird, and a number of students can act as the various dinosaurs.

Name ______________________  Date ______________________

**ACTIVITY**

# HOW CAN YOU MAKE TIME STAND STILL?

Directions: Each of the numbered statements is a saying about time. Choose the correct words from the "Word Box" to complete those sayings to find out just what you have to do to make time stand still. Write the word in the blank, then copy the marked letters in each word in the blank at the bottom of the page for your answer. Not every word will be used.

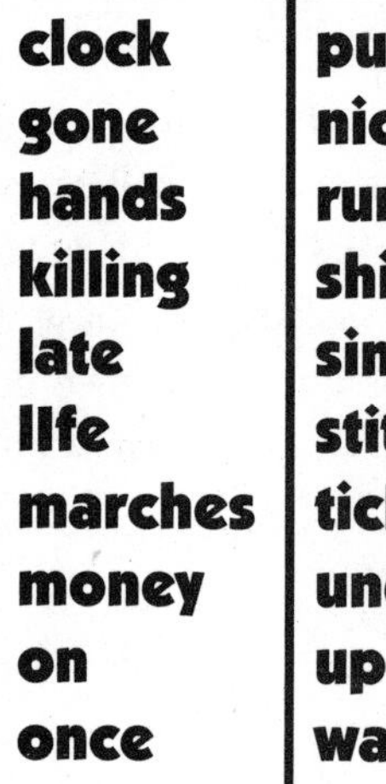

| | |
|---|---|
| clock | punch |
| gone | nick |
| hands | runs |
| killing | shine |
| late | single |
| life | stitch |
| marches | ticks |
| money | under |
| on | up |
| once | waste |

1. Time ___ ___ ___ ___ ___ ___ (___) on.
2. A ___ (___) ___ ___ ___ ___ in time saves nine.
3. Time is ___ (___) ___ ___ ___.
4. Time's ___ (___).
5. It's just a ___ ___ ___ (___) ___ of time.
6. Too much time on your (___) ___ ___ ___ ___.
7. Time to rise and ___ ___ ___ ___ (___).
8. ___ ___ (___) ___ upon a time.
9. Having the time of your (___) ___ ___ ___.
10. Try to be (___) ___ time for once.
11. In the ___ ___ (___) ___ of time.
12. (___) ___ ___ ___ ___ ___ ___ time.

You must ___ ___ ___ ___  ___ ___ ___  ___ ___ ___ ___ ___.

Name ____________________ Date ____________________

**ACTIVITY**

# TIME SAVERS

Directions: Do you have enough time to get everything done that you are expected to do and still have time to do what you want to do—like watching television or interacting with the computer and still having time to do homework? Think of ways you can save time during school days, on weekends, and on vacation. Use the space below to make your list. Include the number of minutes or hours that you will save. When you have added up all of the time saved, explain how you are going to use that time.

| | Your List | Time Saved |
|---|---|---|
| **1.** | ____________ | ____________ |
| **2.** | ____________ | ____________ |
| **3.** | ____________ | ____________ |
| **4.** | ____________ | ____________ |
| **5.** | ____________ | ____________ |
| **6.** | ____________ | ____________ |
| **7.** | ____________ | ____________ |
| **8.** | ____________ | ____________ |
| **9.** | ____________ | ____________ |
| **10.** | ____________ | ____________ |

Total time saved ____________

I will use the time I save to ________________________________________

________________________________________________________________

________________________________________________________________

Name ______________________ Date ______________________

**ACTIVITY**

# I SAW A ____________________!

Directions: Listen to the poem, "I Saw a Brontosaurus," then write your own poem or story about something you have seen or would like to see. Use the outline below to write down your thoughts. Draw a picture of what you have described at the bottom of the page

What I saw was a ____________________ when it suddenly appeared at (on) ________________.

I thought it seemed funny that it was there because ______________________________.

I was surprised at its size since most of them are ______________________________, and it is

______________________________________________, and to be able to see it clearly I had to

______________________________________________. The only thing we could do

together was ______________________________________________

______________________________________________.

It was/was not a lot of fun since it ______________________________________.

People who saw us together said ______________________________________.

Our adventure ended when ______________________________________

and that's all there is to tell about what "I Saw."

This is a picture of IT!

AUTHOR:

**Vera B. Williams**

STANDARD:

**Problem Solving, Numbers and Numeration**

CONCEPT:

**Addition and Subtraction, Estimation, Patterns**



**Materials:**

- Cuisenaire® rods and/or color tiles
- "How Many in the Jar?" activity sheet
- "When Can I Buy That Chair?" activity sheet
- "No Cross Words Here" activity sheet
- Large glass jar
- Jelly beans or other materials to put in the jar
- "Be a Copycat" (optional) activity sheet

# A CHAIR FOR MY MOTHER

The mother in this story works hard as a waitress and needs a comfortable easy chair in which to relax after she comes home from work. The family lost all they had in a fire more than a year ago, and ever since then, they have been saving money in a big jar to buy a chair that is "just right." Friends, relatives, and neighbors have given them the other things they need, such as pans and dishes, a kitchen table and three chairs, a bed, and even a stuffed bear for the young girl—but they do not have a soft chair. One evening the mother announces that the jar is full and they all hope that there is enough money in it for the chair they need. The girl counts the coins and places them in brown wrappers for five cents, ten cents, and quarters. They take the coins to the bank and exchange them for ten-dollar bills. Then they go shopping. They go to four furniture stores and sit in all of the chairs. Each has to make sure they find the one that is most comfortable. When they find their perfect chair, they take it home and place it beside the window with the red and white curtains. In the daytime, the grandmother sits in it and talks to the people passing by, and in the evening, the girl and her mother are very comfortable sitting in it together.

## Introduction

Before reading the story, ask the following:

1. What is a diner?
2. Has anyone ever eaten in a diner? When and where?
3. What kind of food could you order in a diner?
4. The girl in the story once peeled all of the onions for onion soup. Would you like to do that? Why or why not?
5. Does someone in your house have a special chair to enjoy? Do you?
6. Is anyone else allowed to sit in that chair? What happens if someone does?

Share the book, and then lead into the mathematics activity with these questions:

1. Have you ever saved money in a jar or piggy bank?
2. Have you ever saved the money to buy something special? What?
3. Could you tell how much money you had without taking it out and counting it?
4. Can anyone think of a way to estimate the contents of a jar without counting what is inside? Think about it in your groups.

## Mathematics Activity

The "How Many in the Jar?" activity requires students to find ways of making an estimate of the contents of a jar like the one in the story. They should work in small groups of four to plan their problem-solving approach. Each group should write a plan and compare it with that of another group. Each group then carries out the plan and arrives at a solution, also comparing the solution with that of other groups. They should apply Pólya's problem-solving approach (Pólya, G. *How to Solve It,* Princeton: Princeton University Press, 1957) which is:

1. Understanding the problem: Re–state it, decide what is asked, what more you need to know
2. Devise a plan: A visual model, work backwards, simplify the problem, guess, use logical reasoning
3. Carry out the plan: Does the plan work?
4. Look back: Are all questions answered reasonably? More than one solution?

## Follow-Up Activities

The activity sheet "When Can I Buy That Chair?" involves the students in basic addition and subtraction problems using the Cuisenaire® rods. If students name the rods correctly in this self-checking exercise, the answer to this question is revealed.

"Be a Copycat" focuses on the recognition and replication of various patterns using tiles. After students study the different kinds of patterns and designs in the book, they should create some original designs while working in groups. Then groups can see if they can copy other groups' patterns.

The crossword puzzle activity sheet "No Cross Words Here" focuses on the words associated with events in the story. It tests listening and reading skills as well as literal interpretation. The word box lists all of the words needed to complete the puzzle. Students may benefit by working together in pairs. A short discussion of the events that take place in this story will serve to refresh students' memories in preparation for this activity.

Name

Date

# HOW MANY IN THE JAR?

Directions: What is the best way to determine how many are in the filled jar without counting the contents? Follow the problem-solving steps on this sheet. When you are finished, compare your plan with that of another group.

### Step One

Show you understand the problem. Do you need more information? What? ____________________

__________________________________________________

### Step Two

Think of a plan to solve the problem. ________________________________

__________________________________________________

### Step Three

Carry out your plan. What happened? Why did it (or did it not) work? ____________________

__________________________________________________

### Step Four

Look back. Is there more than one solution? ______________________________

__________________________________________________

Which group had the best plan? ____________________________________

Why was that plan the best? ______________________________________

Name ______________________ Date ______________________

ACTIVITY

# WHEN CAN I BUY THAT CHAIR?

Directions: Choose a rod from your set of Cuisenaire® rods to solve the problems. Print the name of the rod in the blank. Copy the marked letters in the blank spaces at the bottom of the page to find the answer to "When Can I Buy That Chair?"

**When this color rod is added to the**

1. blue rod, the sum is 15.
   (_) _ _ _ _ _ _ _ _ _
2. red rod, the sum is 12.
   (_) _ _ _ _ _
3. black rod, the sum is 10.
   _ _ _ _ _ _ _ _ _ _ (_)
4. light green rod, the sum is 11.
   _ _ (_) _ _

**When this color rod is subtracted from the**

5. blue rod, the difference is 8.
   _ _ _ (_) _
6. orange plus yellow rods, the difference is 13.
   _ _ (_)
7. two orange rods, the difference is 11.
   _ _ _ (_)
8. orange plus blue rod, the difference is 15.
   _ _ _ _ (_) _
9. two dark green rods, the difference is 5.
   _ _ (_) _ _
10. two black rods, the difference is 9.
    (_) _ _ _ _ _
11. three yellow rods, the difference is 8.
    (_) _ _ _ _
12. two blue rods, the difference is 14.
    _ (_) _ _ _ _

**When this color rod is added to the**

13. orange plus black rods, the sum is 22.
    (_) _ _ _ _ _
14. three red rods, the sum is 12.
    _ _ _ _ _ _ _ _ (_)
15. brown rod, the sum is 18.
    (_) _ _ _ _ _
16. two black rods, the sum is 22.
    _ _ _ (_) _

**The answer is**

_ _ _ _ _ _ _ _ _ _ _ _ _

_ _ _ _ _ _!

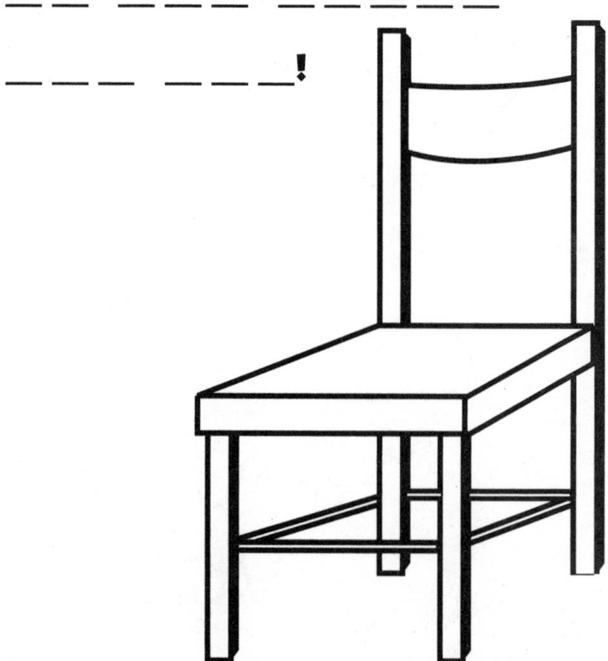

Name

Date

ACTIVITY

# NO CROSS WORDS HERE

Directions: The clues on the next page all refer to an event that takes place in the story *A Chair for My Mother*. They are not written in the order in which the events happened, so be careful. The word box at the bottom of the page lists all of the words you will need to fill in the spaces in the puzzle. If you cannot remember all that happened in the story, look at the book again.

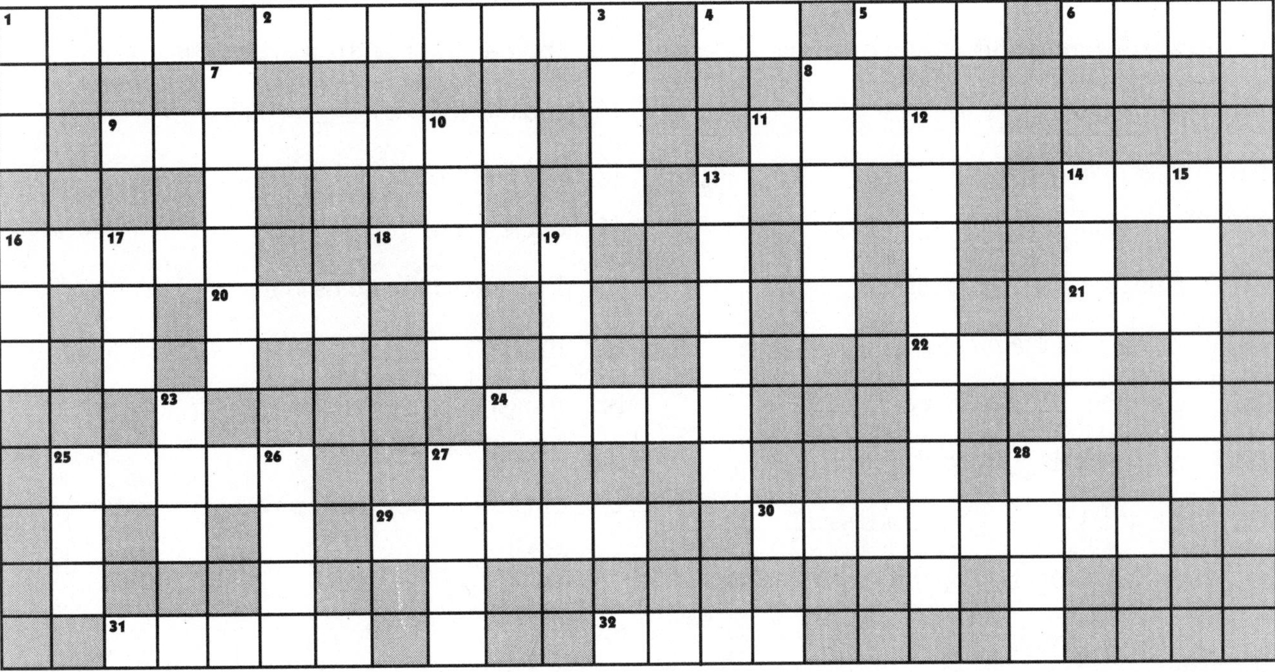

| | | | | |
|---|---|---|---|---|
| **aunt** | **dime** | **money** | **rug** | **tired** |
| **bank** | **diner** | **mother** | **shoes** | **to** |
| **bear** | **fire** | **neighbors** | **sit** | **waitress** |
| **bed** | **flames** | **nice** | **smoke** | **window** |
| **cat** | **home** | **not** | **sofa** | |
| **chair** | **jar** | **out** | **soft** | |
| **coins** | **kitchen** | **quarters** | **store** | |
| **count** | **lost** | **ride** | **ten** | |

## Clues For "NO CROSS WORDS HERE"

### Across

1. They wanted a chair that was _____
2. They were given a _____ table
4. They took the coins _____ the bank
5. Neighbors gave them a _____
6. They lost everything in the _____
9. The mother worked as a _____
11. The girl liked to _____ the money
14. One of the coins put in the jar
16. How the mother felt after work
18. A piece of furniture lost in the fire
20. The firemen put the fire _____
21. The grandmother was _____ hurt
22. The uncle took their chair _____
24. They went to the furniture _____
25. The mother needed an easy _____
29. They took the _____ to the store
30. The highest value of the coins saved
31. They had bought _____ the day of the fire
32. The coins were traded for bills at the _____

### Down

1. They had to _____ in every chair
3. Everyone was _____ to them
7. The new chair is next to a _____
8. The tips put in the jar were all _____
10. _____ from the fire filled the house
12. _____ helped them start over again
13. _____ were shooting high in the air
14. Where the mother worked
15. The daughter of the grandmother
16. A dime is worth _____ cents
17. The grandpa gave them a _____
19. Uncle's wife
23. They saved the coins in a _____
25. The girl's _____ was safe
26. The girl was allowed to _____ in the pickup beside the chair
27. Everything they owned was _____ in the fire
28. What the cousin gave the girl to replace the one lost in the fire

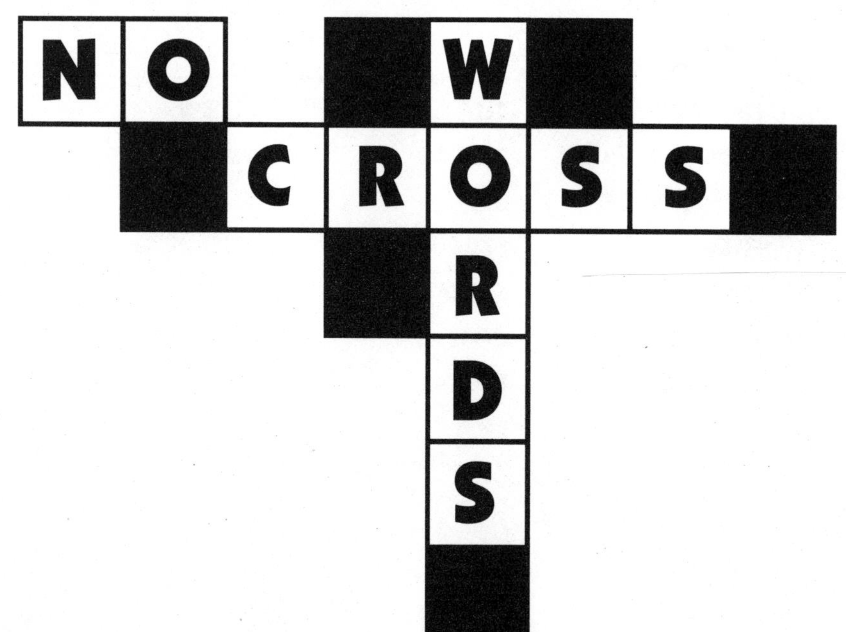

Name ____________________  Date ____________________

**ACTIVITY**

# BE A COPYCAT

Directions: Create three different patterns of any design with your color tiles. Trace just the outline of your figures so that the individual tiles do not show. Then give your paper to a member of another group to see if he or she can duplicate the design. Try copying someone else's design.

| | | | | | |
|---|---|---|---|---|---|
| | | | | | |
| | | | | | |
| | | | | | |
| | | | | | |
| | | | | | |
| | | | | | |
| | | | | | |
| | | | | | |
| | | | | | |
| | | | | | |
| | | | | | |

# ANNO'S MAGIC SEEDS

AUTHOR:
**Mitsumasa Anno**

STANDARD:
**Problem Solving, Number and Number Operations**

CONCEPT:
**Multiplication, Graphs, Comparisons**

## Materials:

- "Seeds, Seeds, and More Seeds, See All the Seeds" activity sheet
- "The Best Foods—Yours or Mine?" activity sheet
- "What Do You Mean—One Meal a Year?" activity sheet
- "Jack's Real Story" activity sheet
- Counters
- Paper, pencils
- Calculators (optional)

As Jack is traveling along the road one day, he meets a wizard who gives him two large golden seeds. The wizard tells Jack that if he bakes one seed until it turns red and then eats it, it will be the only food he needs for a whole year. The wizard also says that if Jack plants the other seed, it will provide him with two more seeds in the spring. Jack does as he is told, beginning a cycle of eating one seed and planting the other. After a few years he decides to eat something else and plant both seeds. That next year his crop doubles, and by the fifth year, there are thirty-four seeds. Alice comes by to help Jack with the work, and each of them eat one seed and plant the others. In the seventh year they marry, and by then the crop is so large that Jack has to build a storehouse for the extra seeds. The seeds keep multiplying, and in the tenth year, Jack and Alice build a bigger house. Before harvest, though, a hurricane strikes and washes away all but ten seeds that Jack manages to save. The ten seeds are enough for them to begin again. Jack, Alice, and their baby each eat one seed, and Jack plants the rest. He and Alice hope that the plants will grow and yield many more magic seeds.

## Introduction

A pre-reading discussion of the story may be used as a motivator to emphasizing certain points by using the following questions:

1. How many of you know the story of *Jack and the Beanstalk?* (Retell this story to help children's recall and discussion about the similarities and differences in the two stories.)

Use these questions after the sharing of this story and before a second reading:

2. Does anyone believe that there could be a magic seed or kind of food that would keep people from getting hungry all of the rest of the year? Why or why not?
3. If you could only eat one food once each year what would it be? Why?
4. Was Jack somewhat lazy at first? What changed him?
5. Why do you think it took Jack so many years to decide to save two seeds to plant?
6. What else might Jack have done with the seeds?

## Mathematics Activity

After discussing the story, share the book again, stopping at each page where the author has asked questions. Give students time to fill in the spaces in the "Seeds, Seeds, and More Seeds, See All the Seeds" activity sheet. Provide calculators and counters for those who need them. Use different colors to represent ones and tens for clarity in understanding place value.

Students should also record their thinking process used to find the answer. Discuss any differences in the process used after individual calculations are completed and as students are working in pairs or groups to compare their answers. They will need to determine how many fruits appeared, then how many seeds were left to bury after Jack did various things to dispose of them, how many Jack saved from the storm, and how many were left to begin the replanting. Emphasis here is on the thinking process of the students as well as the product. Groups should then report on any differences in reaching the solution as well as comparing answers.

## Follow-Up Activities

Ask students to bring in a variety of "magic" seeds, such as jelly beans, M&M's®, miniature marshmallows, or Life Savers®, or provide these materials for them. Use these for a variety of activities, such as measuring and comparing diameters of different types of "seeds," sorting by size or color, polling the class to determine which of the different types of objects they would like to eat, or the color of "seed" that is their favorite. Students can create graphs to show these favorites.

The "The Best Foods—Yours or Mine?" activity involves students in making comparisons of various foods by reading the packaging labels for each type of "magic" food brought in. They will need to determine which contains the least or most amount of sugar, the lowest and highest fat content, and the fewest or most calories. They should then choose the most healthful food based on this information. After they finish the activity, decide if they may eat the objects used in the experiment.

For an alternate or extended activity, use real seeds for a planting experiment. Have students read the package directions for planting depth, water and sunlight needs, growing time, and height of plant.

A long–term project is to plant the seeds and measure them periodically. Students should keep a chart showing the amount of water used, the cost of fertilizer and its effect on growth, and the effect of direct sunlight, as well as showing plant growth by the week. Or students can design a vegetable or flower garden considering the information on the packets about the height and profusion of the plants, growing and harvesting times, and colors in various rows. Gardening catalogs will be a big help.

The activity sheet "What Do You Mean—One Meal a Year?" is a combined mathematics and language exercise. It involves both creative writing and estimation. Students find their own "magic" food that they only have to eat once a year and tell about the effect it has on them and their families regarding what it is, the cost, and so on.

LANGUAGE

"Jack's Real Story" is a writing activity in which students may work individually, in pairs, or small groups to write a short story from Jack's viewpoint. The statements should reveal what Jack is thinking and later, after he meets Alice, their dialogue as the seed crop keeps flourishing. Students should share stories with the class. Choose two of them to be dramatized with class members portraying the Wizard, Jack, Alice, wedding guests, the baby, and people at the market. Students will need a day or more to prepare their skits. Props and music will add to the effectiveness of the presentations.

Name

Date

ACTIVITY

# SEEDS, SEEDS, AND MORE SEEDS, SEE ALL THE SEEDS

Directions: Listen to the story again and use this chart to fill in the numbers to answer the questions about how many seeds were produced, eaten, and planted beginning with the first year after Jack planted both seeds. Be sure to make notes at the bottom of the page on how you arrived at each answer. Use your counters or a calculator if you need to make sure of your calculations.

Counters representing the ones digits must be one color, those representing the tens digits a different color.

SEEDS

| Year | Seed Crop | Seeds Eaten | Seeds Buried | Seeds Stored | Seeds Sold |
|---|---|---|---|---|---|
| One | 4 | 1 | 3 | | |
| Two | 6 | 1 | 5 | | |
| Three | 10 | 1 | 9 | | |
| Four | 18 | 1 | 17 | | |
| Five | | | | | |
| Six | | | | | |
| Seven | | | | 16 | |
| Eight | | | | 34 | 60 |
| Nine | | | | 51 | 100 |
| Ten | | | | | |

Name

Date

ACTIVITY

# THE BEST FOODS—YOURS OR MINE?

Directions: You and a partner will be comparing the "magic" seeds each of you brought to class by reading the information on the labels. Then decide which of these foods is the most healthy. Explain why you reached this decision. Compare your results with another pair of students, then share your information with the whole class.

Use the sentences below to help you in your selections.

My food has:

1. __________ grams of fat.
2. __________ sugar content.
3. __________ number of calories for a serving size of __________.
4. a sodium content of __________________________.

My partner's food has:

1. __________ grams of fat.
2. __________ sugar content.
3. __________ number of calories for a serving size of __________.
4. a sodium content of __________________________.

The most healthful of these two foods is ______________________ because ______________________

______________________________________________________________________.

We agree that the food we like best is ____________________ because ______________________

______________________________________________________________________

The "best" food to eat is ______________________________________________.

Name ______________________  Date ______________________



# WHAT DO YOU MEAN— ONE MEAL A YEAR?

Directions: After hearing Jack's story about his magic seeds, you hunted until you found the same kind of magic food of your own that you eat only once a year. Use the space below to tell how this has changed your life and that of your family.

Was I ever happy when I found that eating ______________________ just once a year would keep me and my family from being hungry the rest of the time. I'm glad it is ______________________ because I ______________________.

The amount each of us eats is ______________________ and costs just ______________________ each day. I can earn the money to pay for it by ______________________.

There is a problem, though, since this "magic" food ______________________.

If I can't find a way to ______________________, it will probably ______________________.

If this doesn't work I will have to ______________________.

Can you think of anything to help me? ______________________

Name ______________________ Date ______________________

**ACTIVITY**

# JACK'S REAL STORY

Directions: Write down Jack's story for him. This is all he has told you: "By now you must know about my meeting the wizard and getting the magic seeds. Well, let me tell you that my life became pretty exciting after that. Here's what happened."

The first thing that I thought when I met him and heard what he said was ______________________________

______________________________________________________________.

But I decided to give it a try and, what do you know, he was right! Eating only one seed once a year was

kind of strange at first, but I ______________________________

______________________________________________________________

and I had more time to ______________________________.

I decided to plant both seeds one year because I ______________________________.

I was glad when Alice stopped to help me so I told her, "______________________________

______________________________________________________________."

When there were so many more seeds she said, "______________________________

______________________________________________________________."

Everything was going fine for us until one day when ______________________________.

We were scared and I yelled to Alice, "______________________________"

while I tried to ______________________________.

When the storm was over I said to Alice, "______________________________"

so we will be "______________________________

And from then on we______________________________.

# SYLVESTER AND THE MAGIC PEBBLE

AUTHOR:
**William Steig**

STANDARD:
**Numbers and Number Sense, Whole Number Operations, Problem Solving**

CONCEPT:
**Addition Combinations**

## Materials:

- Calculators
- "Work Your Own Magic!" activity sheet
- Transparency of "Work Your Own Magic" activity sheet
- "How to Get Rich Quick" activity sheet
- "Sylvester's Sad Situation" journal entry sheet

Sylvester, a very appealing young donkey who loves to collect pebbles, goes off on a rainy Saturday morning to explore the hillside for others to add to his collection. He finds a beautiful red one and discovers it is not only beautiful, it has the magic power of granting any wish he makes as long as he is touching it. He begins to walk home, thinking of all of the good that he can do for others, and does not notice the lion coming his way until they are face-to-face. Sylvester panics and wishes to be turned into a rock—and he is! The magic pebble, however, is lying on the ground next to the rock, so there is no way Sylvester can make his wish to be turned back into himself. When he doesn't return home, his parents are frantic. They search everywhere for him, but of course, he is not found. The seasons come and go, and there is Sylvester, a solitary rock, with no possibility of being restored to his own self. One nice day his parents take a picnic to Strawberry Hill, not knowing that Sylvester (as a rock) is there. His father sees the pebble, places it on the rock that they are using as a table, and wishes Sylvester was with them. Sylvester joins in that wish, and, since the pebble is touching the rock (Sylvester), the wish is granted! The reunited family takes the pebble home and locks it away in a safe place to use later. They already have the best wish of all—Sylvester's return.

## Introduction

Introduce the book by saying that it is a story about a donkey who loves to collect pebbles and about what happens when he finds a very unusual one. Precede the reading of the story by using the following questions to generate interest and elicit a discussion:

1. Is there such a thing as a "magic" power?
2. Have you ever heard of an object with magic powers?
3. What stories do you know about these kinds of objects?
4. Have you ever found or seen a magic object? When or where?
5. Are the stories about objects with magic powers just make-believe? How do you know?

After reading the book, show the pictures again and talk about the many details this illustrator includes in his illustrations that enable the reader to see the emotions of his characters.

## Mathematics Activity

Read the directions on the "Work Your Own Magic!" activity sheet to the students and work through an example with them to ensure their understanding on how to fill in the cells in the chart. A transparency of the chart will be helpful to clarify the procedure. For example, if they believe that statement 1 is true, they should write the number 16 in cell 1; if they think it is false, they should write the number 3 in cell 1, and so forth. Explain that if they fill in the cells correctly, they will find out why this is called a "magic sums" chart. Students may work individually or in cooperative groups if their work is to be compared with and evaluated by their peers.

## Follow-Up Activities

The "How to Get Rich Quick" activity sheet requires students to decide what is the best method for calculating the right combination of lemonade and cookies that will make the most money. They will be deciding what steps the children should take in making the decision. Encourage students to imagine they are about to set up a stand themselves. They are not required to do calculations, only to record the steps in their thinking as they make certain decisions. Provide information on costs and quantities to help them, or they may look at grocery store advertisements for this information. Their decisions should include knowing how much to charge for the lemonade and the cookies as well as how much lemonade to mix and how many cookies to bake.

"Sylvester's Sad Situation" is a writing assignment for students who must imagine how Sylvester feels during certain time periods and seasons when he is imprisoned as a rock. Students will write these "remembered" thoughts as journal entries from their own or Sylvester's viewpoint. Students must relate Sylvester's thoughts and feelings to their own lives as if they would go through these periods all alone. Students may work in pairs if they wish.

Name ______________________ Date ______________________

ACTIVITY

# WORK YOUR OWN MAGIC!

Directions: Read each of the following statements. If you think the statement is true, write the number in the "True" column in the cell named to the left of the statement. If you think the statement is false, write the number in the "False" column in the cell named. When you have filled in all of the cells, read the directions under the square. You may find a surprise!

| Cell | Statement | True | False |
|---|---|---|---|
| (1) | Collecting pebbles is fun for Sylvester. | 16 | 3 |
| (2) | He went out in the rain to look for special pebbles. | 2 | 11 |
| (3) | Sylvester found out that the pebble had magic powers. | 3 | 8 |
| (4) | Seeing the lion did not surprise Sylvester. | 15 | 13 |
| (5) | The wish made by Sylvester was a good one. | 9 | 5 |
| (6) | The lion turned Sylvester into a rock, then left him alone. | 1 | 11 |
| (7) | The rock was a good, safe hiding place. | 4 | 10 |
| (8) | Sylvester, as the rock, couldn't touch the pebble. | 8 | 5 |
| (9) | Sylvester's parents were not worried about him. | 11 | 9 |
| (10) | He called and called for help, but no one heard him. | 2 | 7 |
| (11) | A wolf curled up on him and went to sleep. | 14 | 6 |
| (12) | Sylvester slept through the seasons. | 12 | 16 |
| (13) | His parents took a picnic to Strawberry Hill. | 4 | 12 |
| (14) | When the pebble was on the rock, Sylvester made his wish. | 14 | 10 |
| (15) | His parents scolded him for staying away so long. | 6 | 15 |
| (16) | They used the pebble to make a wish for money. | 13 | 1 |

| | | | |
|---|---|---|---|
| (1) | (2) | (3) | (4) |
| (5) | (6) | (7) | (18) |
| (9) | (10) | (11) | (12) |
| (13) | (14) | (15) | (16) |

Add the numbers in each row, each column, and both diagonals. If you wrote the right numbers in the cells, you will see why it is called a "magic sums" chart.

Why is it called this? ______________________________.

Name ____________ Date ____________

ACTIVITY

# HOW TO GET RICH QUICK

Directions: On a hot summer day, Aaron and Katie hit upon the idea of setting up a stand in their front yard to sell lemonade and cookies. They need you to help them figure out just the right combination of lemonade and cookies that will make the most money. Lead them through the steps that will help them decide. If you do a good job, they may take you to the pool with them.

## The Lemonade and Cookie Problem

If they sell one cookie with every cup of lemonade, how can they decide how much they should charge for each cup and each cookie? Tell them how they can find out.

1. The first thing they should do is ____________________

2. When they know that, they can ____________________

3. Then they can figure ____________________

4. After that, they can ____________________ by

5. What else will they need to know? ____________________

6. How much money will they need to earn to pay for all three of you to go to the pool? ____________________

Name

Date

# SYLVESTER'S SAD SITUATION

Directions: Sylvester was a rock for a very, very long time, and it was absolutely impossible for him to talk to anyone, so to help pass the time, he began to think about all that he was missing back home. Help him get those thoughts down on paper. Try to remember everything he might have thought about during that time and make his journal entries for him by using this outline.

**Week one:** ______________________________

______________________________

**Month one:** ______________________________

______________________________

**Thanksgiving:** ______________________________

______________________________

**December holidays:** ______________________________

______________________________

**Spring comes:** ______________________________

______________________________

**Summer again:**

At last! My family finds me and I am myself again! We couldn't be any happier than we are right now.

AUTHOR:
**Chris Van Allsburg**

STANDARD:
**Problem Solving, Reasoning, Geometry**

CONCEPT:
**Number Operations, Logical Conclusions, Coordinate Points**



# JUMANJI

Peter and Judy become bored while staying home alone one afternoon, and they decide to explore the park. Peter finds an interesting-looking box, a game called "A Jungle Adventure Game." A note attached to the bottom of the box warns them that the game is not for everyone, and that it is very important to play the game to its conclusion once it has been started. Messages written on colored squares lead from the start deep in the jungle to the city of Jumanji. Peter's roll of the dice lands him on the square that shows a lion ready to spring. When he looks at Judy, he is surprised to see a look of absolute horror on her face. He turns and sees what she has—a lion on top of their piano, ready to spring! From that point on, whatever is shown on a square they land on appears right in the house! Judy finally rolls a twelve, which takes her to Jumanji and finishes the game. Luckily, everything in the house reverts to the way it was before the game began. They pack the game back in the box, hurry to the park with it, return home, and, tired out, fall asleep. When their parents and guests arrive home, they try to explain what they have been through. Mrs. Budwig is convinced that they imagined the whole episode. Later, Peter and Judy see Mrs. Budwig's two sons, who never follow game instructions, carry the game home with them.

## Introduction

The statements on the "Probable and Improbable Events" activity sheet serve as an introduction to this book and this type of literature. Hold a discussion of the statements before reading the story. Then introduce the story as one in which some rather improbable events take place and how lucky the children in the story were to solve the problems these events caused. As you read the statements, have students label each statement as a P (probable) or an I (improbable) event in the blanks on the sheet.

## Materials:

- "Probable and Improbable Events" activity sheet
- "Name the Character" activity sheet
- "Find the Hidden Name" activity sheet
- Straight edges and pencils
- "A Most Unusual Game!" activity sheet

## Mathematics Activity

Give each student a copy of the activity sheet titled "Name the Character." Review the directions with the class before anyone begins. If the students have not had a lot of practice plotting coordinates, guide them through the process. Working in pairs or in small groups will be helpful. Use a transparency of the grid for a whole-class activity. Students may take turns locating points and drawing lines. If this activity seems too complicated for some students, vary it by either limiting the plotting of the points to just those that give the shape of the head of the character, stopping after point (11, 16), or to have those points outlining the body already connected.

## Follow-Up Activities

Give each student a copy of the "Find the Hidden Name" activity sheet. They may work in pairs in locating the points and filling in the letters. Those who finish before the allotted time limit may create a graph of their own for challenging other students. Their graphs may focus on a wide variety of names, related to their interests or to some topic being studied in the classroom rather than on this particular story.

On the "A Most Unusual Game" sheet, students should write a story about their favorite game. The story must include a description of what would happen if the characters and events in the game came alive as they do in the "Jungle Adventure" game of Jumanji. This is a great exercise for stretching the imagination by connecting the activity to an ordinary event or interests in the lives of the students. It may be a board, card, video, or CD-ROM game. The game may be one they have played, one they would like to play, or one they make up. It may also be a variation of the "Jungle Adventure" game. The writing may be fun to do in cooperative groups of four or in pairs so they can share ideas.

Name

Date

# PROBABLE AND IMPROBABLE EVENTS

Directions: Read each of the following statements and decide if it is a probable (likely to happen) event, or an improbable (not likely to happen) event. Write a P for the probable events and an I for an improbable event in the blank at the end of the statement.

1. Characters from a book come to life and talk to each other after everyone in the house has gone to sleep. _________

2. Animals carry on conversations among themselves but are careful to keep this a secret from humans. _________

3. You will eat at a fast-food restaurant sometime this month. _________

4. A stranger will come up to you on the street and give you ten million dollars. _________

5. You will need a new pair of sneakers this year. _________

6. You will have some homework to do this week. _________

7. A game can have magical powers. _________

8. You can grow wings and fly if you wish hard enough. _________

9. You will have to take at least one test in school this month. _________

10. You will want to watch at least one program on TV this week. _________

List one probable and one improbable event that might happen in your life this year.

Probable event ________________________________________

Improbable event ________________________________________

Name

Date

# NAME THE CHARACTER

Directions: Locate the coordinate points and connect them to find one of the very important characters in the story, *Jumanji.*

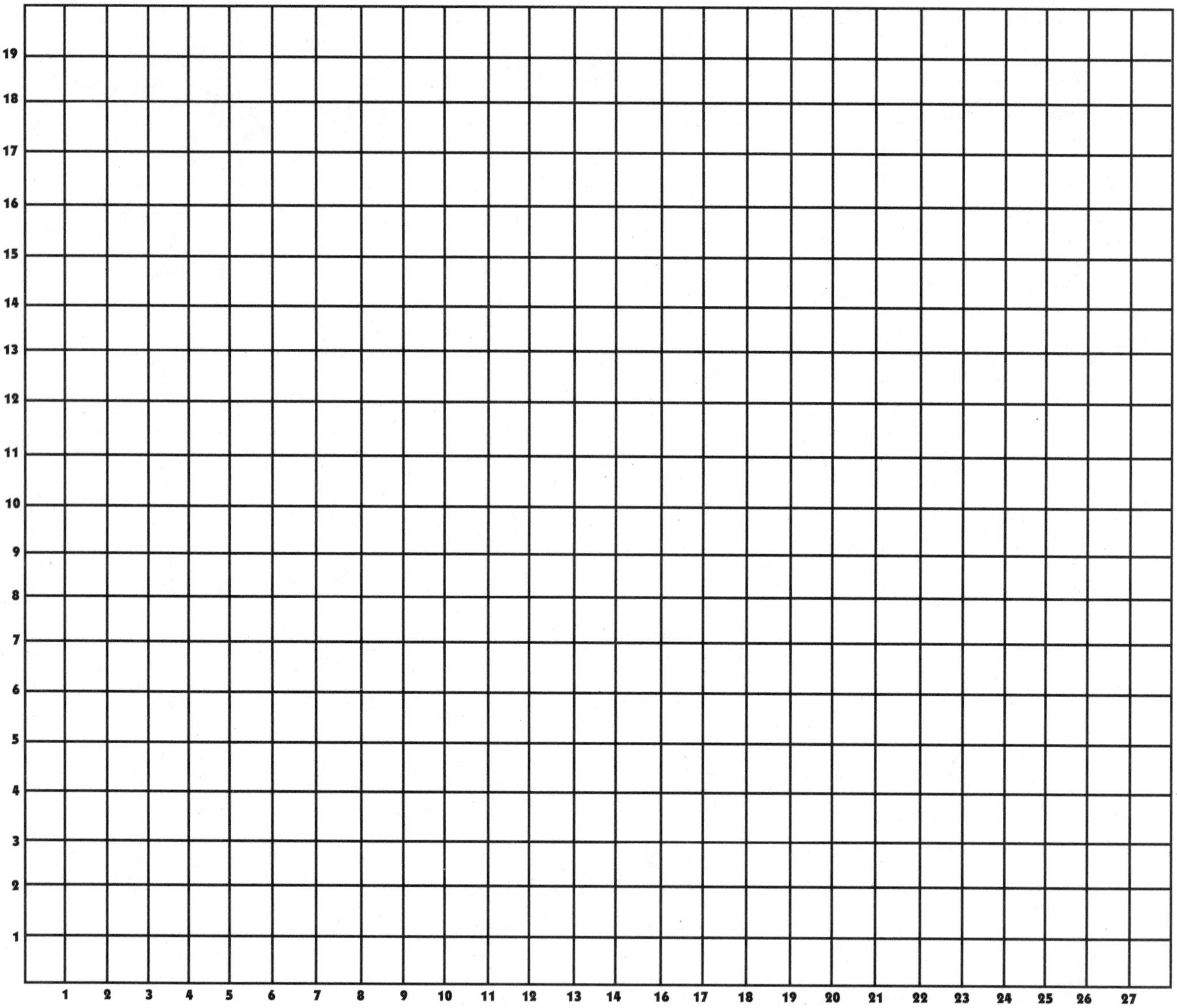

(11,6) (9,4) (9,7) (8,5) (7,7) (6,6) (3,6) (1,7) (1,8) 2,9) (2,12) (1,13) (1,15) (2,17) (6,19) (8,19) (6,16) (10,18) (8,14) (11,16) (9,13) (12,10) (23,10) (25,9) (26,1) (24,7) (24,3) (22,1) (19,1) (19,2) (20,2) (22,3) (22,6) (13,6) (12,1) (9,1) (9,2) (10,2) (11,6)

**The Character is the**______________________________

Name ____________________ Date ____________________

**ACTIVITY**

# FIND THE HIDDEN NAME

Directions: Identify the coordinate points in the correct order—the first number is the row across the bottom, and the second number is down the side—to discover the name of one of the most interesting characters in this story. Use the grid below to locate the squares with the letters in them. Write the letters in the blank over the specified coordinate points to find the name of the character.

| 10 | W | | | T | | | D | | | L | |
|---|---|---|---|---|---|---|---|---|---|---|---|
| 9 | | B | | | | | | | R | | |
| 8 | | | N | | E | | | G | | | |
| 7 | | | | Q | | | O | | | | |
| 6 | S | | J | | | V | | | | C | |
| 5 | | K | | | M | | | | | | R |
| 4 | | | | H | | | | | P | | |
| 3 | | I | | | | | | U | | | Y |
| 2 | X | | | | | O | | | | | |
| 1 | | | E | | | | | | | F | |
| | 1 | 2 | 3 | 4 | 5 | 6 | 7 | 8 | 9 | 10 | 11 |

____ ____ ____ ____ ____ ____ ____ ____ ____ ____

**(9,9) (4,4) (2,3) (3,8) (6,2) (10,6) (3,1) (11,5) (7,7) (1,6)**

Draw a picture of this character in the space below.

Name

Date

# A MOST UNUSUAL GAME!

Directions: Think about your favorite game and imagine what might happen if, when you play it next time, it turns into a game like the one in *Jumanji*. Develop a plan to leave the game safely, then decide what you would say to someone who wants to play your game after you have finished it.

My favorite game is ______________________________.

When I was playing it one day, something very surprising happened. All of a sudden ______________________________

______________________________

and ______________________________.

I didn't know what to do at first, then I ______________________________

______________________________.

Bad luck! That didn't help, so I had to ______________________________

______________________________.

By then I was getting tired, but I knew that if I just kept playing I could ______________________________

______________________________.

At last the game ended and I felt ______________________________.

I left a note with the game telling the next player to ______________________________.

AUTHOR:
**Beverly Cleary**

STANDARD:
**Number Operations, Problem Solving, Mathematics as Communication**

CONCEPT:
**Multiplication and Division, Data Analysis**

**Materials:**

- Calculators
- "Guess How Many Are Coming to Dessert" activity sheet
- "Are All the Wheels on the Bus?" activity sheet
- "A la 'Ramona Quimby, Age 8'" activity sheet
- Name tags or labels (optional)
- Markers or crayons



# RAMONA QUIMBY, AGE 8

The irrepressible Ramona is excited and happy about becoming a third-grader. At the same time, her father is excited and happy to re-enter college to earn a teaching degree. Things go well at school for Ramona until the day she follows the lunchroom tradition of smacking a hard-boiled egg on her head to crack it. When she does, she discovers it is not even a little bit boiled—and her hair is an awful mess. As if that weren't enough, she overhears her teacher labeling her "a nuisance." One day she gets sick at school and feels she has disgraced herself by throwing up in her classroom. She stays home the next day, feeling sorry for herself, but is cheered up when a friend brings her letters from the class. She gets an idea for her book report on *The Left-Behind Cat* from a television commercial for cat food, and it is a big hit. This gives Ramona the courage to ask her teacher why she considers Ramona a nuisance. She finds out that the teacher meant that getting the egg out of her hair was the nuisance, not Ramona. One November afternoon when everyone is feeling gloomy, Mr. Quimby decides it will cheer them up to go out to dinner. An elderly man thinks they are a nice family, and he pays for their meal. This helps them realize that even with all of their problems, they are a nice family, for they all love and take care of one another.

## Introduction

Most students will have some acquaintance with the Ramona books by now, so the activities can be used without a pre-reading activity, either with the class organized in small groups or with the whole class participating at the same time. Use these questions to refresh memories about Ramona:

1. How many of you know who Ramona Quimby is?
2. Does Ramona get into trouble sometimes? Is it always her fault?
3. What kinds of things does Ramona do that cause trouble for her?
4. Does she always seem to come out on top?
5. Why do you think this happens?
6. Do you know anyone who is like Ramona? (Make sure no names are mentioned.)
7. This book about Ramona begins the day she enters third grade. As you listen to it, decide if you felt the same way she does when you were about to begin your first day in third grade.

Read the book to the class or, if there are multiple copies, set up peer reading sessions.

## Mathematics Activity

Ramona and her sister had to cook dinner one night for the family. They had some problems with having the right number of ingredients for the recipes. The problem for the students in the activity "Guess Who's Coming for Dessert" is to modify the recipe in two ways: for half as many and twice as many people. This is best done as a small group activity with each group member responsible for an assigned part of the ingredients.

## Follow-Up Activities

The "Are All the Wheels on the Bus?" activity sheet involves students in comparing the time it takes each of them to get to school in the morning and home in the afternoon. Information is charted to show how many walk to school and how many come on a bus and how many come by different transportation. Students make time comparisons by the length of the morning and afternoon times spent in riding the bus and to determine if the ride takes a longer time one way or another.

Ramona likes to write her full name followed by "Age 8," and writes it that way on the label for her jar of fruit fly larvae. She also decorates the label by drawing very small fruit flies on it. Students can do something similar by using the "A la Ramona Quimby, Age 8" activity sheet. They need not write their ages after their names, but they should choose something that they like that tells a good thing about themselves or describes a hobby, or something they like to do. Once they design their name tags, they should write an explanation of why they chose what they did to describe themselves.

An extension of this activity is to write the characteristic on one side of the name tag and their name on the other. The characteristics are then displayed on a bulletin board entitled, "Do You Know This Person?" Make a sheet available for students to write their guesses of the names of classmates they think fit the characteristic. Hold a contest to show who made the most correct guesses.

Name ____________________ Date ____________________

ACTIVITY

# GUESS HOW MANY ARE COMING FOR DESSERT

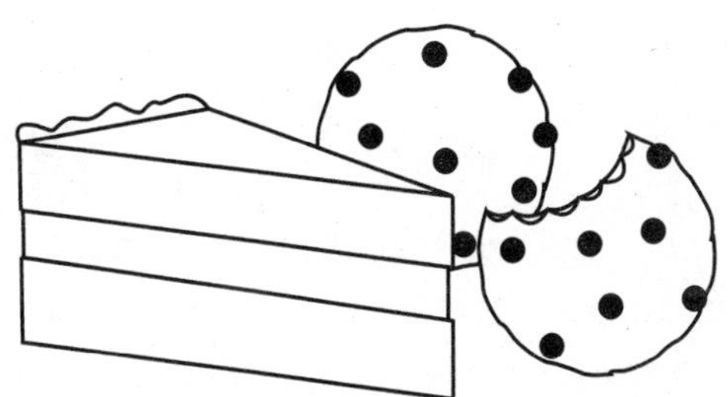

Directions: You are going to be cooks, just like Ramona and Beezus. A group of your very best friends are coming for dessert. The recipe you will use is shown below, but it is for ten people. You have to change it since the group you have to feed has four people. You do such a good job they decide to come back the second night. They show up with fifteen friends, so you have to change the recipe again. Don't forget to include yourself—you won't want to miss this wonderful treat!!



**Recipe For "Dessert Delight"**

Serves ten

| | |
|---|---|
| 2 cups dragon's toenails, finely ground | 480 ml dragon's toenails, finely ground |
| 1 cup green slime | 240 ml green slime |
| 4 tablespoons vampire's teeth, chopped | 60 ml vampire's teeth, chopped |
| 2 teaspoons witch's hair | 10 ml witch's hair |
| 6 tablespoons moldy cobwebs | 90 ml moldy cobwebs |
| A pinch of finely ground sneaker lace | A pinch finely ground sneaker lace |

Mix the ingredients together thoroughly in the order given. Pack in an old sock and refrigerate for five hours. Spread on the sole of a sneaker packed with mud and serve on a bed of seaweed. Decorate with sprays of shredded cactus leaves. As your guests taste this delicious concoction they will exclaim in delight and beg you to give them the recipe—but don't do it—well-seasoned sneakers are a delicacy and hard to find.

**Recipe Modifications**

**For four people + the cook**

__ (cup) (ml) dragons' toenails, finely ground

__ (cup) (ml) green slime

__ (tablespoons) (ml) vampire's teeth, chopped

__ (teaspoon) (ml) witch's hair

__ (tablespoons) (ml) moldy cobwebs

__ (pinches) finely ground sneaker lace

**For nineteen people + the cook**

__ (cup) (ml) dragons' toenails, finely ground

__ (cup) (ml) green slime

__ (tablespoons) (ml) vampire's teeth, chopped

__ (teaspoon) (ml) witch's hair

__ (tablespoons) (ml) moldy cobwebs

__ (pinches) finely ground sneaker lace

Mix, refrigerate, and serve as directed in the original recipe.

Recipe comments____________________________________________.

Name ______________________ Date ______________________

ACTIVITY

# ARE ALL THE WHEELS ON THE BUS?

Directions: There are many different ways of getting from home to school and back again. You are to do two things: 1) find out how many in your class walk to school and how many ride, and 2) how many ride the bus and how many ride there in something else. Determine how to gather this information and how to show the results of what you have gathered.

**A. Ways of Gathering Information**

1. Walkers ______________________
2. Riders ______________________

**Ways of Showing Information** ______________________

______________________

**B. Ways of Gathering Information**

1. Bus Riders ______________________
2. Others ______________________

**Ways of Showing Information** ______________________

______________________

**C. Ways of Gathering Information about Time Spent in Traveling**

1. Walkers ______________________
2. Riders ______________________

**Ways of Showing Information about Time Spent in Traveling** ______________________

______________________

Name

Date

# A LA "RAMONA QUIMBY, AGE 8"

Directions: In the space on this sheet, write your name a la (in the way) that Ramona Quimby, Age 8, does. Write something about you, *instead of your age,* after your name. It may be something about what you like to do, to eat, where you like to go, a sport you like, something you do very well, or your position or age in your family. Then decorate the name tag as Ramona did on the one she put on her fruit fly larvae jar. You may write something about you on just one side of the paper and your name on the back of it so that each of your classmates can try to guess who it is that the name tag describes. Write a sentence or two on this page explaining why you chose to write what you did.

**Name** ______________________________

I chose to write my name this way because it ______________________________.

If I could change anything about my name it would be to ______________________________.

AUTHOR:
**Sid Fleischman**

STANDARD:
**Problem Solving, Reasoning, Measurement**

CONCEPT:
**Number and Number Sense, Logical Conclusion, Computation**

## Materials:

- "Worth Your Weight in What?" activity sheet
- "Follow the Clues" activity sheets: "The First Missing Number," "The Second Missing Number"
- "Descriptive Names" activity sheet
- A supply of nickels and a bag of jumbo marshmallows for each group
- Several kitchen scales or balances
- Calculators

# THE WHIPPING BOY

Prince Brat, as he is called throughout the kingdom, delights in making life miserable for the people of his father's court. He is so disruptive that a whipping boy has be brought to the castle to be punished for the prince's incessant misbehavior. Jemmy, a homeless boy taken from the streets to serve as that boy, is the son of a rat catcher and has spent much of his life in the sewers under the city streets. He finds some advantages in living in the castle and would enjoy it if not for the constant whippings. Prince Brat eventually becomes bored with castle life and decides to run away, but not alone. He commands Jemmy to go with him. Jemmy intends to slip away from the prince as soon as it becomes dark, but they are captured by two outlaws. The outlaws plan to hold the boys for ransom, but Jemmy, followed by the prince, manages to escape. They are pursued by the outlaws in what turns out to be a dangerous chase. After a harrowing episode in the sewers, Prince Brat decides it is time to go home. Jemmy fears the king will punish him, but the king rewards him instead. Most importantly, the prince has grown up, and, in changing his values, has earned Jemmy's trust and friendship.

## Introduction

Explain that the way in which Jemmy was treated by the king was accepted in the time period in which this story takes place but that such behavior is no longer tolerated. Before reading the story, tell students that they are to listen for some of the unusual characters' names and to try to remember them. Ask the following questions:

1. How many of you would like to be chosen to live in a royal palace and be a companion to a prince (or princess) who is just your age? Why or why not?
2. What do you think are some of the things you would be allowed to do there?
3. What would be the best thing about living in a castle?
4. Would there be anything that might not be good about being chosen? Explain your answer.

After sharing the book, review these questions and ask if any students would change their minds about living in a castle.

## Mathematics Activity

The outlaws first decided to ask for the prince's weight in gold. Then Jemmy influenced them to ask for more. Students are going to determine an approximate value of their weight in nickels and in marshmallows (or other materials) and decide which of these they would prefer to have. For a hands-on activity, supply about ten nickels and a bag of marshmallows for each group of four or five students. Also give each group a kitchen scale or balance and a copy of the activity sheet "Worth Your Weight in What?" Students will need to use calculators. In some instances, students may need to be taken through this activity one step at a time. If using money is not practical, other materials—jelly beans, marbles, etc.—are appropriate substitutes.

## Follow-Up Activities

The two "Follow the Clues" activity sheets enable students to become detectives, as they must examine clues to find two missing numbers, "The First Missing Number" and "The Second Missing Number" (in a way that the king would have searched for the prince) who have run away from King Googol. This is best done in a group learning situation. Students must sort some extraneous clues from useful ones before they find a solution. Once this activity has been completed, groups should develop their own set of clues (on a smaller basis) and challenge other groups to find a solution.

Give students the "Descriptive Names" activity sheet as a guide for writing hyphenated names to describe a personality trait of the various characters. Introduce it with a brief discussion about the unusual names in the story—Hold-your-nose-Billy and Captain Hot-Hot-Potato. Point out that the names describe a characteristic or something about the character and that is what the students are to do in filling in the activity sheet. One or two examples may be done with the whole class (or group) to get the activity started.

Name ____________ Date ____________

ACTIVITY

# WORTH YOUR WEIGHT IN WHAT?

Directions: Find the approximate value of your weight, not in gold, but in nickels and marshmallows. Then decide if you want to be given your weight in nickels or in marshmallows. The final step is done for you on the chart.

Follow these steps using nickels:

Write your weight in the blank. I weigh ______ pounds (or ______ kilograms).

**Step one:** Place nickels on a scale until you have close to 0.11 pounds (or 50 grams) of weight (about 10). Find how many nickels equal 1.1 pounds (500 grams) by multiplying the number of nickels by ________ . _______ nickels weigh 1.1 pounds (or 500 grams).

**Step two:** Multiply the number of nickels by _______ to find how many weigh 2.2 pounds (or 1,000 grams—1 kilogram). _______ nickels weigh 2.2 pounds (or 1 kilogram).

**Step three:** Multiply the number of nickels by _______ to find their money value and write that number in the blank ______ . Then use the chart to find the value of your weight in money.

| **Pounds** | **Kilograms** | **Money** | **Number** |
|---|---|---|---|
| 22 | 10 | $100 | 1400 |
| 33 | 15 | $200 | 2100 |
| 44 | 20 | $300 | 2800 |
| 55 | 25 | $400 | 3500 |
| 66 | 30 | $500 | 4200 |

My weight is worth $ ______. My weight is worth _______ marshmallows.

Follow these steps using marshmallows:

**Step one:** The number of marshmallows in 1.1 pounds (or 500 grams) is about 70.

**Step two:** Multiply the number of marshmallows by _______ to find the number of marshmallows in 2.2 pounds (or 1 kilogram) and write that number in the blank. ______

Find the number of marshmallows equal to your weight and write that number in the blank under the chart. How long would it take you to eat that many? ______

I would like to have my weight in ______ because ____________________________________________.

Name

Date

# FOLLOW THE CLUES

Directions: Prince Brat's father (or his advisors) didn't seem to be very good at following clues as they hunted for the missing boys. It is your turn to follow clues since King Googol, one of the greatest number of all the numbers, has asked for your help. Two numbers are missing from the kingdom of Number Land. If that were not bad enough, no one can figure out just which two. That is your job, and a big job it is!

## The First Missing Number

**Clue number one:** The number in the thousands place is the highest number on a die.

Deduction: This number is ________.

**Clue number two:** The number in the hundreds place is the remainder when the number of dwarfs Snow White met is multiplied by 4 and divided by 6.

Deduction: This number is ________.

**Clue number three:** It is a four-digit number.

Deduction: Now I know ____________________________________________.

**Clue number four:** The number in the tens place evenly divides 10, 35, and 45.

Deduction: Easy. This number is ________.

**Clue number five:** There are three even numbers and one odd number.

Deduction: This tells me ____________________________________________.

**Clue number six:** When the number is reversed and added to itself the sum is 8,998.

Deduction: Well, the number in the units place plus the number in the thousands place = 8, so the number in the units place is ________.

All of these clues together tells me that the number is ________.

## The Second Missing Number

Directions: Follow these clues in the same way as you did for the first missing number. King Googol will be very happy and reward you when he hears that both of the missing numbers have been found. He may even give you your own place in the royal palace!

**Clue number one:** The number in the thousands place evenly divides 14, 35, and 56.

Deduction: this number is ______.

**Clue number two:** The number in the hundreds place is three times the number of bears seen by Goldilocks.

Deduction: Easy! This number is ____________.

**Clue number three:** It is a four-digit number.

Deduction: That lets me know ________________________________________________.

**Clue number four:** When the digits in the number are reversed and added to the original number the sum is 9,218.

Deduction: Okay, the number in the units place plus the number in the thousands place = 8, so the number in the units place is _______.

**Clue number five:** There are two even numbers.

Deduction: This helps me to ________________________________________________.

**Clue number six:** The number in the tens place is the difference between the numbers in the thousands place and the hundreds place.

Deduction: The number is _______.

Putting all of the clues together I know that this number is ______.

The two missing numbers are _________ and _________, and if they ever run away again,

King Googol will have to send someone else to find them!

Name ____________________ Date ____________________

ACTIVITY

# DESCRIPTIVE NAMES

Directions: If you have read many of Sid Fleischman's stories, you know he likes to have fun with the names of his characters such as Hold-your-nose-Billy and Captain-Hot-Hot-Potato. Be just like this author and think of that kind of a name for each person listed below.

| **Character's Description** | **Character's Name** |
|---|---|
| Max is always munching nachos. | ____________________ |
| Juan hates having homework. | ____________________ |
| Sally despises spinach. | ____________________ |
| Ray is an expert on roller blades. | ____________________ |
| Tina loves to trick people. | ____________________ |
| Sara is a great soccer player. | ____________________ |
| Pete is a talented card player. | ____________________ |
| Susie's six siblings are sisters. | ____________________ |
| Gerald has a German Shepherd puppy. | ____________________ |
| Ramona reads a lot of books. | ____________________ |
| Lucy likes to lift weights. | ____________________ |
| Shawn loves to solve story problems. | ____________________ |
| Now, think of a name for yourself! | ____________________ |

AUTHOR:

**Dianne Snyder**

STANDARD:

**Problem Solving as Communication**

CONCEPT:

**Whole Number Operations, Estimation, and Computation**

# THE BOY OF THE THREE-YEAR NAP

Taro is a lazy, sleepy boy who is known throughout the village as "the boy of the three-year nap." His poor mother is at her wit's end, for no matter how she begs him, he will not do anything to help her. Then a rich merchant builds a beautiful twenty-room house in town, complete with a garden, pond, and teahouse. Taro is fascinated with all of this luxury and develops a plan to marry the daughter of the merchant. He asks his mother to make an outfit for him without revealing what he intends to do with it. One night he disguises himself as the patron god of the village, confronts the merchant, and demands that he allow his daughter to marry Taro (him) or he (the god) will turn her into a clay pot. The unhappy merchant goes to Taro's mother to ask for her consent to the forthcoming marriage. She understands what Taro has done and makes some demands of her own in order to have her house improved. Last of all, she asks for a job for Taro. Once all of her demands are met, the marriage is set. Taro's job of counting sacks of rice for his father-in-law keeps him busy, but he seems happy enough. He is never called "the boy of the three-year nap" again.

## Introduction

Before sharing this story, inform the class that since the setting of the story is Japan, there may be some words that may be unfamiliar to them. Students will need to listen and try to determine what they mean by how they are used in the context of the story. After sharing the story, distribute the "Vocabulary Reference" activity sheet to students. Students should work in pairs or groups of four. If there are questions about the meaning of other words, add them to the list. Review and discuss this activity after everyone finishes it. It provides an excellent preparation for the activity sheet "Mother Knows Best."

## Materials:

- "Vocabulary Reference" activity sheet
- "Sleepy Time" activity sheet
- "Rice Is Nice" activity sheet
- "Mother Knows Best" activity sheet
- Calculators

## Mathematics Activity

"Sleepy Time" focuses on the idea of how much time people spend sleeping. Students first estimate how many hours Taro would have slept in one week if no one had awakened him, then how long he would sleep for a year, then three years. Then they will estimate these time spans in relation to each of the others. Students are also asked to think of a process to use in finding out the number of hours Taro would sleep if he slept twenty-four hours a day for three years (assume that each year is comprised of 365 days). Calculating a solution is optional. The second part involves students in keeping track of the number of hours of sleep they get each night for a two-week period. A table is provided to record these hours. This information is used to determine, in a general sense, the average number of hours they would sleep in one night. Then they can calculate the number of hours they would sleep in a week, year, and three years. A comparison can then be made between the number of hours they would sleep and those that Taro would sleep in a three-year nap. This is best carried out in a group format after the information on the table has been filled in, as some students may not be able to work independently on this activity.

## Follow-Up Activities

The "Rice Is Nice" activity involves students in attempting to solve the problem of the best and easiest way to measure how many pounds (or grams) of rice fill a sack so Taro can find out just how rich he is. This allows practice in problem-solving rather than in finding one correct way of counting rice. Cooperative learning groups work best for this activity. Supermarket ads will aid students in estimating the cost of one pound (or 454 grams) of rice, or the price may be set beforehand.

"Mother Knows Best" extends the students' comprehension and retention of vocabulary from this story as they fill in the blanks with the coded answer. If needed, they may use the vocabulary reference sheet as a help. This is a self-checking activity with a coded message at the bottom of the sheet.

Name ______________________ Date ______________________

ACTIVITY

# VOCABULARY REFERENCE

DIRECTIONS: Look at the list of words from the story *The Boy of the Three-Year Nap*. Write what you think is the meaning of each one, trying to remember the context in which each word was used. Work with a classmate. If you are still not exactly sure you have the right definition, find the word in the dictionary.

| | Context Clue | Definition |
|---|---|---|
| 1. Brocade | ______________ | ______________ |
| 2. Carp | ______________ | ______________ |
| 3. Cormorant | ______________ | ______________ |
| 4. Ujigami | ______________ | ______________ |
| 5. Ivory | ______________ | ______________ |
| 6. Kimono | ______________ | ______________ |
| 7. Obis | ______________ | ______________ |
| 8. Samurai | ______________ | ______________ |
| 9. Shrine | ______________ | ______________ |
| 10. Teahouse | ______________ | ______________ |

Use this space to list any additional words in the story that are new to you.

______________________ Name

______________________ Date

**ACTIVITY**

# SLEEPY TIME

Directions: Taro would have slept for three years if no one had awakened him. How many hours do you think he would have slept in three years? How many hours do you think you sleep each night? Each week? How many hours do you think you would you sleep in three years? Now can you find out! Read on!

### Your Estimate:

If Taro sleeps 24 hours a day he would sleep

_____ hours in 1 week _____ hours in 1 year _____ hours in 3 years

If you think you sleep ____ hours each night, you sleep

_____ hours in 1 week _____ hours in 1 year _____ hours in 3 years

Circle how much longer Taro would sleep than you

just as long 2 times as long 3 times as long 4 times as long 5 times as long

How can you find the number of hours Taro would sleep in three years?

### Keeping Track

Directions: Write the number of hours you sleep each night for 2 weeks in the table, then add them all together. Divide the sum by 14 for a general idea of the "average" number of hours slept in one night. Multiply by 7 to find how many hours you sleep per week. Fill in the number of hours you can sleep in 1 year and 3 years by filling in the blanks below the table.

| | Sun. | Mon. | Tues. | Wed. | Thurs. | Fri. | Sat. |
|---|---|---|---|---|---|---|---|
| **WEEK** | | | | | | | |
| **One** | | | | | | | |
| **Two** | | | | | | | |

_____ hours in 1 week _____ x 52 = hours in 1 year _____ x 3 = hours in 3 years_____

Circle how close you were to estimating how much longer Taro would sleep than you.

just right close not very close way, way off—asleep

_________________________ Name

_________________________ Date

**ACTIVITY**

# RICE IS NICE

Directions: Taro has the job of counting rice sacks for his rich father-in-law and he wants to know how much each sack is worth once it is filled. He needs you to carry the sacks to market for him, so it's important to know how heavy a sack you can carry. Estimate this, then determine how to find the cost per pound (or grams) of rice. Then calculate how much each sack is worth when it is filled. Work with a partner or small group to find a way to solve this problem.

**Step 1:**

How can you find out how heavy a sack you can carry?
We could carry a sack that weighs
about __________ pounds (or grams).

**Step 2:**

Once we know how heavy a sack can be carried, we need to find ______________________________

_________________________________________________________________________.

**Step 3:**

We can find that out by ______________________________________________________

_________________________________________________________________________.

**Step 4:**

So far we have found out that ______________________________________________.

**Step 5:**

All that we have to find out now is how much ___________________________________

and we can do that by ____________________________________________________.

**Step 6:**

Our answer is that each sack of rice is worth about _________________________________.

Name ____________________

Date ____________________

ACTIVITY

# MOTHER KNOWS BEST

Directions: The word box at the bottom of the page contains words that are in the story *The Boy of the Three–Year Nap.* Choose a word from this box that best completes each sentence. Then copy the marked letters in the blanks below the word box to find out why "Mother Knows Best."

| **brocade** | **kimonos** | **merchant** | **rooms** | **sleep** | **wed** |
|---|---|---|---|---|---|
| **cormorant** | **mansion** | **rice** | **shrine** | **teahouse** | **work** |



1. Taro's mother wants him to get a job, but he refuses to (__) __ __ __.
2. The rich merchant built a twenty-room __ __ __ __ __ (__) __.
3. Taro confronted the merchant at the __ __ (__) __ __ __.
4. The poor widow worked all day sewing (__) __ __ __ __ __ __ __ for rich people.
5. Taro earned his nickname because all he did was __ __ __ (__) __.
6. The merchant didn't want his daughter to __ __ (__) Taro.
7. The women in the merchant's family wore gowns of (__) __ __ __ __ __ __.
8. Taro finally wound up counting sacks of __ __ __ (__).
9. There was a (__) __ __ __ __ __ __ __ __ __ on the grounds of the merchant's land.
10. Many a __ __ __ __ __ __ __ __ (__) fished in the Nagara river.
11. The __ (__) __ __ __ __ __ __ __ __ believed he was visited by Ujigami.
12. Taro's mother was glad when more (__) __ __ __ __ were added to the small house.

**Her plan** __ __ __ __ __ __ __ __ __ __ __ __ __ __ **than Taro's.**

AUTHOR:

**Cynthia Rylant**

STANDARD:

**Problem Solving, Measurement, Estimation Mathematical Terms**

CONCEPT:

**Number Operations, Distance and Time**

## Materials:

- "Travel Time" activity sheet
- Maps for each small group
- 10 pieces each (a total of 30) of 2" by 3" (5 cm by 7.5 cm) tagboard in three different colors for Game One
- 10 pieces of green, 10 pieces of yellow, 10 pieces of blue, 10 pieces of red, 10 pieces of orange, and 10 pieces of gray for Game Two and Game Three (60 cards of 6 different colors)
- Directions for making the "Greet Your Relatives" games
- Rules for the "Greet Your Relatives Game One," "Greet Your Relatives Game Two," and "Greet Your Relatives Game Three"
- "My Best—or Worst—Visit" activity sheet
- Calculators (optional)

# THE RELATIVES CAME

**The family members travel a long way from their home in Virginia to spend time with relatives. When they arrive, everyone is so overjoyed to see everyone else that the next several hours are filled with people just hugging each other. There are so many people in the house that supper must be eaten in shifts and there are not enough beds to go around. They fall asleep wherever space is available in a great tangle of arms, legs, and bodies. As the visit continues, the out-of-town relatives pitch in and help with the chores and fix anything that needs fixing. They also share the fun of playing games and are involved in so many enjoyable activities that there is little time left to think of their return trip home. The day does come, however, when they must leave. The old station wagon is packed up again in preparation for the long drive home. The families take leave of each other with promises of another get-together soon. The host family begins to miss their visitors immediately, but the prospect of their upcoming trip to Virginia helps them feel less lonesome. Their visiting relatives are glad to return home and soon become too busy harvesting grapes to be sad.**

## Introduction

Before sharing the book with the class, ask the following:

1. Do you have any relatives who live far away from you? Where?
2. Does your family ever visit them? Do they come to visit you? How often?
3. Is there plenty of room for all of the people in the house? What do you do if there isn't?
4. Have you ever stayed with relatives for almost the whole summer? What kinds of things did you do?

Explain that the story is about two families visiting each other during the summer, the kinds of things they did together to have fun, and ways in which they helped each other. After sharing the story, ask:

1. Was the family in the book anything like your family? In what way?
2. Would you like to have that many extra people in your house all at once? Why or why not?
3. How would you feel about having so many people in your room that you would have to sleep on the floor?
4. The visiting family had to travel a long way to get to the home of the relatives. Have you ever had that kind of long trip? When?

This last question leads into the mathematics activity "Travel Time," in which the students take an imaginary trip.

## Mathematics Activity

"Travel Time" involves the students first in estimating how long it will take to make a trip to visit a "relative" in another state. As the trip proceeds, they are given number of delays which will slow the trip. They must calculate, then subtract time taken for the various delays that are described on the activity sheet from their estimated arrival time. Departure and arrival destinations are assigned for each group according to the particular kind of map given to them.

## Follow-Up Activities

The three different versions of the "Greet Your Relatives Game" use mathematical terms instead of words as students try to find the relationship between questions and answers. Question and answer cards are in three categories: Computation, Measurement, and Geometry. There are three ways to play this game, going from simple rules to more complex ones. A run-through demonstration of each game may be needed.

**Version One:** Write questions and answers on one card within each category. Separate categories by using three different colors of tagboard or by labeling the top of the cards as "C," "M," or "G." Shuffle cards within each category and place them facedown in three separate stacks on the playing surface. The game is played in the manner of "Trivial Pursuit" as a player draws a card from his or her own choice of category without looking at it and tries to answer the question as it is read to him or her by the player on the right. If the correct answer is given the player answering is declared a "relative" and earns 4 points. If the player does not give the correct answer, he or she is declared "not a relative" and earns no points. The player places the card facedown at the bottom of the deck and play goes to the next player. The player with the most points is the winner.

**Version Two:** The game may be played as a "Concentration" game by an individual or in pairs. In addition to separating the cards into three categories, separate them into questions and answer cards by color. All cards in each category are placed facedown on the playing surface in a single layer (question cards and answer cards) one category at a time. Players turn over two cards at a time to see if they match. If they do, the player keeps the cards. If not, he or she turns the cards facedown again. The winner is the player with the most matches at the end of the game. Students may choose how many categories to play.

**Version Three:** Separate cards into three categories, using two different colors within each category for the question and answer cards. Students play as partners. The game is played in three rounds, by category. Players have to choose a different category each time. One partner draws a question card and the other partner draws an answer card. If partners agree that the two cards match (if the question is answered on the answer card), they declare themselves "relatives." If not, they declare themselves "strangers." Each player earns 4 points for the correct response. Cards are placed facedown at the bottom of the deck and play goes to the next set of partners. Partners with the highest number of points win. A time limit may be set.

The "My Best—or Worst—Visit" involves students in describing a visit they remember as their best or worst visit. This could have been with a friend or relative and may have taken place at the student's home or that of the other person or persons. If they do not remember a specific visit, they may write about an imaginary one.

Name ____________________ Date ____________________

ACTIVITY

# TRAVEL TIME

Directions: Your place of departure and arrival is marked on your map. Look at the scale on the map to find out how many miles you will be traveling on the trip. Estimate and record how long the trip will take driving at the speed of 65 miles (or 104 kilometers) per hour. Read each of the delays listed below and estimate the number of minutes each will take. Subtract that number from the total time estimated. How close you were to your estimated arrival time?

## Estimates

You leave your house at 6:30 A.M. and plan to drive straight through with only a few stops. Your trip is ________ miles/kilometers as read on the map scale. Traveling at the speed of 65 miles (104 kilometers) per hour, it will take you ________ hours to get there, so your estimated arrival time is __________.

## Delays

1. You stop for breakfast at your favorite fast-food restaurant. This takes __________ minutes.

2. After you have driven for 30 miles (48 kilometers), your little sister begins to cry because she left her favorite toy back at the restaurant. Going back for it takes __________ minutes.

3. After driving for another hour, you come to road construction and are stopped for twenty minutes in a traffic tie-up.

4. By this time everyone is beginning to get hot and thirsty, so you stop at a rest area for something cold to drink. You are there ________ minutes.

5. Just as it seems you are going to make up for lost time, you hear a strange noise under the car. It takes ________ minutes to remove a long tree branch stuck there.

6. Everything goes well for the next hour and a half, then some other strange noises are heard—this time inside the car. It is your stomach rumbling—time for food! You have to wait in a long line this time, then wait for a place to sit down, so your meal break takes ________ minutes.

All goes well and you arrive after two more hours of driving. How long was your trip and how close was your original estimate?

Name

Date

ACTIVITY

# "GREET YOUR RELATIVES" GAME CARD DIRECTIONS

"Greet Your Relatives Game One" requires 30 pieces of 2" by 3" (5 cm by 7.5 cm) tagboard in three different colors. Questions and answers given below are written on the same card. The categories are Computation —first color, Measurement—second color, and Geometry—third color, or are identified by a "C," "M," or "G" printed on the top of each card.

"Greet Your Relatives Game Two" and "Greet Your Relatives Game Three" require the use of two different color cards within each of three different categories: green for "Computation" question cards and yellow for answer cards; blue for "Measurement" question cards and red for answer cards, and orange for "Geometry" question cards and gray for answer cards. Copy the following on 60 pieces of 2" by 3" (5 cm by 7.5 cm) pieces of tagboard for Games Two and Three. Cards should be laminated.

| COMPUTATION QUESTION CARDS | COMPUTATION ANSWER CARDS |
|---|---|
| What is the answer to 20 x 40? | 800 |
| When 11 is divided by 3, what is the remainder? | 2 |
| What is 16 divided by 4? | 4 |
| Multiplication is the same as repeated what? | addition |
| Repeated subtraction is the same as what? | division |
| What is the answer to 12 x 10? | 120 |
| 6 + 8 = 8 + 6 is an example of what property? | commutative |
| 22 + 18 + 30 equals what? | 70 |
| What is the product of 9 x 8? | 72 |
| What is the answer to a division problem called? | quotient |

Name

Date

# ACTIVITY

| MEASUREMENT QUESTION CARDS | MEASUREMENT ANSWER CARDS |
|---|---|
| How many dollars are 6 quarters, 4 dimes, and 2 nickels? | 2 |
| How many quarts are in 1 gallon of milk? | 4 |
| Which is longer, a centimeter or an inch? | inch |
| How many ounces are in 1 pound? | 16 |
| How many cents would you receive in change if you paid for an 87-cent item with a dollar bill? | 13 |
| To what does the number 3.14 refer? | pi |
| What is the perimeter of a 4-inch/10 cm square? | 16/40 |
| 212 degrees F equals how many degrees C? | 100 |
| How many feet are in one yard? | 3 |
| What is the area of a 2" by 4"/ 5 cm by 10 cm rectangle? | 8/50 |

| GEOMETRY QUESTION CARDS | GEOMETRY ANSWER CARDS |
|---|---|
| How many sides does a hexagon have? | 6 |
| What shape is the same as a bicycle wheel? | circle |
| What shape is a stop sign? | octagon |
| If you changed a triangle into a figure with six sides, how many more sides would it need? | 3 |
| What is the distance around a figure called? | perimeter |
| How many sides are in a square? | 4 |
| What tool is used to measure an angle? | protractor |
| What is a five-sided figure called? | pentagon |
| What shape does a cereal box have? | rectangle |
| What shape is the honeycomb of a bee? | hexagon |

Name

Date

ACTIVITY

# GREET YOUR RELATIVES GAME ONE

## Rules

This game is for 3 to 4 players. Players choose a category: Computation, Measurement, or Geometry.

Shuffle each stack separately, then placed each facedown in the middle of the table. The player who rolls the lowest number on a die goes first, then play goes to the right around the table.

The first player draws a card from one of the stacks (choosing the category) and keeping it face down so he or she does not see what is on it, hands it to the player on the right. That player reads the question on the card to the player who drew it. If the player gives the correct answer, he or she is declared a "relative" and earns 4 points. If the answer is incorrect, he or she is declared "not a relative" and earns no points.

The card is then placed facedown at the bottom of the deck and the process is repeated going to the right around the table. Players with the highest number of points win the game.

Record your points here: Round one _____ Round two _____ Round three _____

Name ______________________ Date ______________________

ACTIVITY

# GREET YOUR RELATIVES GAME TWO

### Rules

This game may be played alone or with pairs of players.

Choose a category and shuffle the question cards, then the answer cards, keeping them separated.

Lay the question cards and the answer cards facedown in a single layer on the table.

Turn up one question card and one answer card. If the answer seems right for the question card, you have found two "relatives" and you may keep those cards. If the answer doesn't seem right, turn both cards facedown again.

Keep turning up cards, two at a time, until all the relatives have met or until the time limit is up.

The player with the most matches wins the game.

Record your points here: Round one _____ Round two _____ Round three _____

Name ______________________  Date ______________________



# GREET YOUR RELATIVES GAME THREE

**Rules**

4 to 8 people play as partners and the game is played in 3 rounds.

A different category is chosen for each round. Question and answer cards are kept separate.

Cards in each category are shuffled and placed facedown in two stacks separated by color in the center of the table.

The player who rolls the lowest number on a die goes first, then play goes to the right around the table. Partners take turns drawing the first card each time.

Choose a category: Green cards are "Computation" question cards, yellow cards are "Computation" answer cards; blue cards are "Measurement" question cards and red cards are "Measurement" answer cards; orange cards are "Geometry" question cards and gray cards are "Geometry" answer cards.

One partner draws a question card and the other partner draws an answer card (from the same category). If partners agree that the answer card drawn fits the question card they declare the cards to be "relatives." If the two cards do not match, they are declared "strangers." If correct, each player earns 4 points. If incorrect, no points are earned. Cards are then placed face down at the bottom of the deck and play goes to the next set of partners.

Play continues until all of the cards have been drawn or until partners have had an equal number of turns.

Partners with the most points win the game.

Record your points here: Round one _____ Round two _____ Round three _____

Circle the kind of questions that were hardest for you to answer:

**Computation** **Measurement** **Geometry**

Name ______________________ Date ______________________

**ACTIVITY**

# MY BEST—OR WORST—VISIT

Directions: Fill in the spaces below to tell about the very best visit you have ever had with either a friend or a relative. If you cannot remember a "best" visit, tell about the "worst" one. If you have not had either kind, write about a visit you wish you could have had!

1. My (best) (worst) (imaginary) visit was when I saw my ______________________.

2. First of all, we ______________________

   and then after that ______________________.

3. The (most) (least) (hoped for) fun we had was when ______________________

   ______________________.

4. The (most) (least) (imagined) trouble we got into was when ______________________

   but it wasn't my fault and so I ______________________.

5. The next time we see each other, I hope that we ______________________.

6. If we never get to see each other, again I'll feel ______________________.

# Math & Stories

## Answer Key

### Where Should These Animals Be?

1. Tiger C(**I**)RCLE
2. Fox TRIA(**N**)GLE
3. Snake HEXAG(**O**)N
4. Mouse SQ(**U**)ARE
5. Ox (**R**)ECTANGLE
6. Deer HEA(**R**)T
7. Goat OCTAG(**O**)N
8. Monkey (**O**)VAL
9. Lion DIA(**M**)OND

Where should these animals be? **IN OUR ROOM.**

### Name That Number Now

1. 3
2. 6
3. 2 + 2 hands + 2 + 2 feet = 8
4. 1
5. 7
6. 10
7. 1 mouth + 3 bears = 4
8. 10 toes – 1 = 9
9. 5
10. 2

### Mother Goose Counts to Ten

1. two
2. nine
3. eight
4. one
5. six
6. three
7. ten
8. four
9. seven
10. five

### Simple Simon's Problem

1. yellow + black
2. purple + brown
3. white + purple + black
4. light green + blue
5. white + dark green + yellow
6. dark green + dark green

### More or Less

1. less
2. more
3. more
4. less
5. less
6. less
7. less
8. less
9. less
10. more
11. less
12. more
13. less
14. more
15. more
16. more
17. more
18. more

### The (Fish) Eyes Have It

1 + 2 = 3
3 + 3 = 6
6 + 4 = 10
10 + 5 = 15
15 + 6 = 21
21 + 7 = 28
28 + 8 = 36
36 + 9 = 45
45 + 10 = 55

**55 FISH EYES**

### Make a Match

1. H
2. F
3. I
4. J
5. C
6. B
7. A
8. D
9. E
10. G

### How Many Mice Are Left?

1. 7 – 1 = 6
2. 7 – 4 = 3
3. 7 – 7 = 0
4. 7 – 6 = 1
5. 7 – 5 = 2
6. 7 – 3 = 4
7. 7 – 2 = 5

## Find the Hidden Words

Answers may vary. Here are some suggestions.

**Strawberry**

**Two-letter words:**

As

At

**Three-letter words:**

| | |
|---|---|
| Art | Say |
| Awe | Set |
| Bat | Tab |
| Bay | Tar |
| Ear | Tea |
| Eat | War |
| Rat | Was |
| Raw | Yes |
| Ray | Yet |
| Sat | |
| Saw | |

**Four-letter words:**

| | |
|---|---|
| Bear | Stay |
| Bray | Sear |
| Read | Tray |
| Rest | Wart |
| Star | Wary |
| Stab | Year |

**More than four letters:**

Stray

Teary

Weary

**Snatcher**

**Two-letter words:**

An

**Three-letter words:**

| | |
|---|---|
| Ant | Hat |
| Are | Her |
| Cat | Tan |
| Has | Ten |

**Four-letter words:**

| | |
|---|---|
| Ache | Nest |
| Chat | Seat |
| Hear | Star |
| Near | |

**More than four letters:**

| | |
|---|---|
| Chant | Snatch |
| Chart | Starch |
| Ranch | Stare |

## Who Is Really the Greatest?

| | | | | | | | | | |
|---|---|---|---|---|---|---|---|---|---|
| 1 | 2 | 3 | 4 | 5 | 6 | 7 | 8 | 9 | 10 |
| | 12 | | 14 | 15 | 16 | 17 | 18 | 19 | 20 |
| | 22 | | 24 | 25 | 26 | 27 | 28 | 29 | 30 |
| | 32 | | 34 | 35 | 36 | 37 | 38 | 39 | 40 |
| 51 | | 43 | | | | 47 | | 49 | |
| 51 | | 53 | | 55 | | 57 | | 59 | |
| 61 | | 63 | | 65 | | 67 | | 69 | |
| 71 | | 73 | | | | 77 | | | |
| 81 | 82 | 83 | 84 | 85 | 86 | 87 | 88 | 89 | 90 |
| 91 | 92 | 93 | 94 | 95 | 96 | 97 | 98 | 99 | 100 |

## Cookie Cooking Counting

| LEMON MOONS | YOUR CHANGES |
|---|---|
| 1 cup of flour | 2 cups of flour |
| 1 teaspoon of baking powder | 2 teaspoons of baking powder |
| 1/4 teaspoon of salt | 1/2 teaspoon of salt |
| pinch of nutmeg | 2 pinches of nutmeg |
| 1 egg | 2 eggs |
| 1/3 cup of cooking oil | 2/3 cups of cooking oil |
| 1/2 cup of sugar | 1 cup of sugar |
| 1 teaspoon of lemon peel | 2 teaspoons of lemon peel |
| 1 teaspoon of lemon juice | 2 teaspoons of lemon juice |
| | |
| 240 ml flour | 480 ml flour |
| 5 ml baking powder | 10 ml baking powder |
| 1.25 ml salt | 2.50 ml salt |
| pinch of nutmeg | 2 pinches of nutmeg |
| 1 egg | 2 eggs |
| 80 ml cooking oil | 160 ml cooking oil |
| 120 ml sugar | 240 ml sugar |
| 5 ml lemon peel | 10 ml lemon peel |
| 5 ml lemon juice | 10 ml lemon juice |

## Follow the Pattern

| | | |
|---|---|---|
| 5 | 7 | 6 |
| 4 | 9 | 2 |
| 1 | 13 | 10 |
| 8 | 11 | |
| 3 | 12 | |

## Folktale Numbers—Lucky Or Not?

1. 3
2. 3
3. 7
4. 7
5. 3
6. 7
7. 4
8. 1, 2, 3
9. 12
10. 3
11. 7
12. 40

## The Lucky(?) Seven

1. A= 2, S = 7 so AS = 9
2. D= 3 A = 2 Y = 9 S = 7 so DAYS = 21
3. E= 3 A = 2 S = 7 Y = 9 so EASY = 21
4. S= 7 A = 2 D = 3 so SAD = 12
5. S= 7 A = 2 T = 8 so SAT = 17
6. S= 7 A = 2 Y = 9 so SAY = 18
7. S= 7 E = 3 A = 2 T = 8 so SEAT = 20
8. S= 7 E = 3 T = 8 so SET = 18
9. S= 7 T = 8 A = 2 Y = 9 so STAY = 26
10. Y= 9 E = 3 S = 7 so YES = 19

The special number is 7.

## Fox Counting

1. 12
2. Father, mother, ten little foxes
3. Answers will vary.
4. Answers will vary.
5. Verse 4? 4 Verse 5? 5
   Verse 7? 7 Verse 3? 3
   Verse 2? 2 Verse 6? 6
6. 1 2 3 4 5 6 7 8 9 10
7. 2 4 6 8 10
8. 10 9 8 7 6 5 4 3 2 1
9. By looking at the illustrations and counting

## Why, You're As Sly As a Fox!

1. bees
2. mule
3. mice
4. bug
5. goose
6. cat
7. kitten
8. swan
9. horse
10. cow

## Riddle Me One, Riddle Me Two

Toad's lost button was: white, round, large, thick. Tell how the buttons found were different from Toad's: black, square, small, thin

Other answers will vary.

## What Shape Is Your Shape?

Sample Shapes:

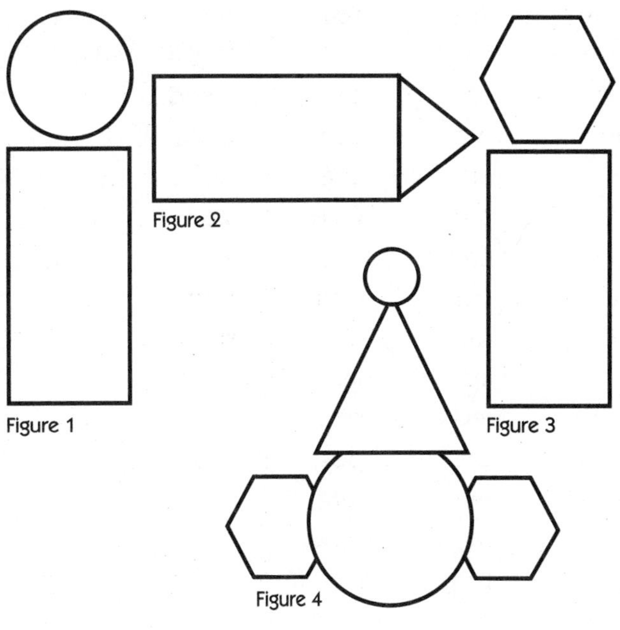


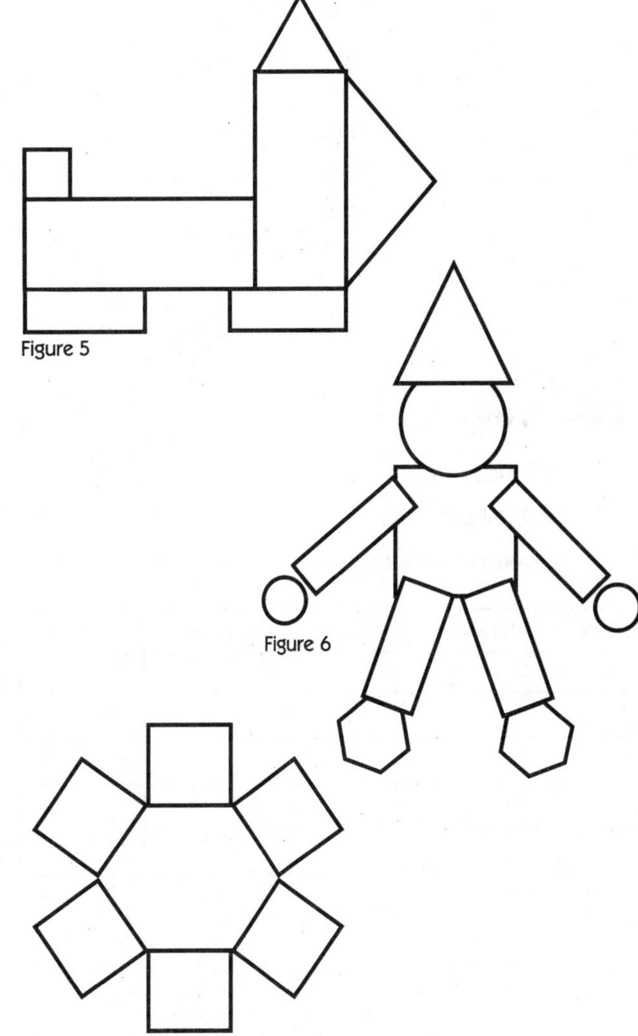

## Are You Money Wise?

Answers may vary. Here are some suggestions.

| **Two** | **Three** | **Four** | **Five** | **More** |
|---|---|---|---|---|
| **2** cents | **4** cents | **6** cents | **8** cents | **12** cents |
| at | air | care | cared | render |
| in | are | cart | delta | taints |
| is | art | cite | point | tender |
| it | ate | coin | stair | trained |
| | cat | cost | stare | strained |
| | cop | dent | start | |
| | den | lend | spire | |
| | ire | lent | | |
| | led | pint | | |
| | oar | post | | |
| | net | rate | | |
| | rat | rend | | |
| | red | rent | | |
| | rip | sent | | |
| | sit | soar | | |
| | sir | spin | | |
| | tar | spit | | |
| | ten | star | | |
| | tin | tent | | |
| | tip | time | | |
| | | tire | | |

## Coin Trading

1. 3, 2 quarters, 1 half-dollar
2. 100, all pennies
3. Answers will vary.

| Pennies | Nickels | Dimes | Quarters | Half-Dollars |
|---|---|---|---|---|
| | | | 2 | 1 |
| 100 | | | | |
| 10 | 1 | 1 | 1 | 1 |
| 5 | 3 | 3 | 2 | |
| | | 5 | | 1 |

## When Are You Coming 'round?

1. **(T)**RAPEZOID
2. HEXAG**(O)**N
3. CUB**(E)**
4. SQU**(A)**RE
5. REC**(T)**ANGLE
6. RHO**(M)** BUS
7. CIRCL**(E)**
8. TRI**(A)**NGLE
9. CYC**(L)**INDER
10. **(S)**PHERE

**TO EAT MEALS**

## Stop Bugging Me!

1. mosquitoes
2. giant water bug
3. bee
4. flea
5. mosquito
6. giant water bug
7. mosquito
8. flea
9. mosquitoes
10. bee

## Let Me Count the Ways

| | **King Lion Calls The** | **Who Says The Trouble-Maker Is The** |
|---|---|---|
| 1. | Mother owl | Monkey |
| 2. | Monkey | Crow |
| 3. | Crow | Rabbit |
| 4. | Rabbit | Python |
| 5. | Python | Iguana |
| 6. | Iguana | Mosquito |

King Lion tells the council that the one who really caused the trouble is the Mosquito because he annoyed the Iguana who then scared the Python who, in turn, scared the Rabbit. She frightened the Crow who startled the Monkey, who killed the owlet. This was the reason that the Mother Owl didn't awaken the sun. Unfortunately, the Mosquito was never found and punished!

## How About Some Scrambled Letters for Breakfast?

1. Monkey
2. Iguana
3. Owlet
4. Snake
5. Crow
6. King Lion
7. Rabbit
8. Mosquito

## The "No Room For Any More" Game

| | | | | | |
|---|---|---|---|---|---|
| 1. 15<br>+50<br>65 | 2. 20<br>+49<br>69 | 3. 59<br>+21<br>80 | 4. 48<br>+36<br>84 | 5. 65<br>+27<br>92 | 6. 37<br>+34<br>71 |
| 7. 26<br>+32<br>58 | 8. 14<br>+13<br>27 | 9. 52<br>+19<br>71 | 10. 17<br>+33<br>50 | 11. 23<br>+49<br>72 | 12. 45<br>+45<br>90 |
| 13. 79<br>–39<br>40 | 14. 68<br>–66<br>2 | 15. 43<br>–28<br>15 | 16. 72<br>–45<br>27 | 17. 59<br>–21<br>38 | 18. 46<br>–19<br>27 |
| 19. 38<br>–9<br>29 | 20. 22<br>–10<br>12 | 21. 99<br>–90<br>9 | 22. 62<br>–29<br>33 | 23. 66<br>–16<br>50 | 24. 22<br>–9<br>13 |

## Daffy Definitions

1. Book Crook
2. Funny Money
3. Sweet Treat
4. Great Skate
5. Wow Cow
6. Noon Room
7. More Shore
8. Norse Horse
9. Dare Bear
10. Bat Cat
11. Near Steer
12. Fun Done

## How Can You Make Time Stand Still?

1. MARCHE(**S**)
2. S(**T**)ITCH
3. M(**O**)NEY
4. U(**P**)
5. WAS(**T**)E
6. (**H**)ANDS
7. SHIN(**E**)
8. ON(**C**)E
9. (**L**)IFE
10. (**O**)N
11. NI(**C**)K
12. (**K**)ILLING

You must

**STOP THE CLOCK**

## When Can I Buy That Chair?

1. (**D**)ARK GREEN
2. (**O**)RANGE
3. LIGHT GREE(**N**)
4. BR(**O**)WN
5. WHI(**T**)E
6. RE(**D**)
7. BLU(**E**)
8. PURP(**L**)E
9. BL(**A**)CK
10. (**Y**)ELLOW
11. (**B**)LACK
12. P(**U**)RPLE
13. (**Y**)ELLOW
14. DARK GREE(**N**)
15. (**O**)RANGE
16. BRO(**W**)N

The answer is **DO NOT DELAY BUY NOW!**

## No Cross Words Here

| S | O | F | T | | K | I | T | C | H | E | N | | T | O | | B | E | D | | F | I | R | E |
|---|---|---|---|---|---|---|---|---|---|---|---|---|---|---|---|---|---|---|---|---|---|---|---|
| I | | | | W | | | | | | | I | | | | C | | | | | | | | |
| T | | W | A | I | T | R | E | S | S | | C | | | C | O | U | N | T | | | | | |
| | | | | N | | | | M | | | E | | F | | I | | E | | | D | I | M | E |
| T | I | R | E | D | | | S | O | F | A | | | L | | N | | I | | | I | | O | |
| E | | U | | O | U | T | | K | | U | | | A | | S | | G | | | N | O | T | |
| N | | G | | W | | | | E | | N | | | M | | | | H | O | M | E | | H | |
| | | | J | | | | | | S | T | O | R | E | | | | B | | | R | | E | |
| | C | H | A | I | R | | | L | | | | | S | | | | O | | B | | | R | |
| | A | | R | | I | | M | O | N | E | Y | | | Q | U | A | R | T | E | R | S | | |
| | T | | | | D | | | S | | | | | | | | | S | | A | | | | |
| | | S | H | O | E | S | | T | | | B | A | N | K | | | | | R | | | | |

## Seeds, Seeds, And More Seeds, See All The Seeds

| Year Seed | Crop Seeds | Eaten Seeds | Buried Seeds | Seeds Stored | Seeds Sold |
|---|---|---|---|---|---|
| One | 4 | 1 | 3 | | |
| Two | 6 | 1 | 5 | | |
| Three | 10 | 1 | 9 | | |
| Four | 18 | 1 | 17 | | |
| Five | 54 | 1 | 33 | | |
| Six | 66 | 2 | 64 | | |
| Seven | 128 | 12 | 100 | 16 | |
| Eight | 200 | 2 | 120 | 34 | 60 |
| Nine | 240 | 3 | 120 | 51 | 100 |
| Ten | | 3 | 7 | | |

## Work Your Own Magic!

| | | | |
|---|---|---|---|
| (1) **16** | (2) **2** | (3) **3** | (4) **13** |
| (5) **5** | (6) **11** | (7) **10** | (8) **8** |
| (9) **9** | (10) **7** | (11) **6** | (12) **12** |
| (13) **4** | (14) **14** | (15) **15** | (16) **1** |

Why is it called this? All the rows, columns, and diagonals add to the same sum: 34.

## Probable And Improbable Events

1. I
2. I
3. P
4. I
5. P
6. P
7. I
8. I
9. P
10. P

## Name the Character

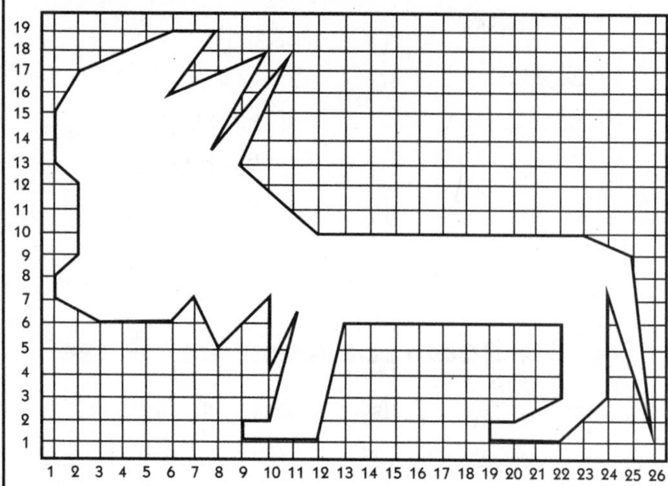

(11,6) (9,4) (9,7) (8,5) (7,7) (6,6) (3,6) (1,7) (1,8) (2,9) (2,12) (1,13) (1,15) (2,17) (6,19) (8,19) (6,16) (10,18) (8,14) (11,16) (9,13) (12,10) (23,10) (25,9) (26,1) (24,7) (24,3) (22,1) (19,1) (19,2) (20,2) (22,3) (22,6) (13,6) (12,1) (9,1) (9,2) (10,2) (11,6)

The character is the lion!

## Find the Hidden Name

Rhinoceros

## Guess How Many Are Coming For Dessert

| FOR FOUR PEOPLE + THE COOK | FOR NINETEEN PEOPLE + THE COOK |
|---|---|
| 1 cup (240 ml) dragon's toenails, finely ground | 4 cups (960 ml) dragon's toenails, finely ground |
| 1/2 cup (120 ml) green slime | 2 cups (480 ml) green slime |
| 2 tablespoons (30 ml) vampire's teeth, chopped | 8 tablespoons (120 ml) vampire's teeth, chopped |
| 1 teaspoon (5 ml) witch's hair | 4 teaspoons (20 ml) witch's hair |
| 3 tablespoons (45 ml) moldy cobwebs | 12 tablespoons (180 ml) moldy cobwebs |
| 1/2 pinch finely ground sneaker lace | 2 pinches finely ground sneaker lace |

## Worth Your Weight In What?

Find out how much you weigh.

Money, step one: 10, 100

Step two: 200

Step three: 0.05, $10.00

Marshmallows, step two: 2, 140

## Follow the Clues: The First Missing Number

Clue number one: This number is 6.

Clue number two: This number is 4.

Clue number three:
Now I know no more than I did.

Clue number four: Easy! This number is 5.

Clue number five: This tells me nothing that will help.

Clue number six: Well, the number in the units place plus the number in the thousands place = 8, so the number in the units place is 2.

All of these clues together tell me that the number is 6,452.



## Follow the Clues: The Second Missing Number

Clue number one: This number is 7.

Clue number two: Easy! This number is 9.

Clue number three: That tells me no more than I knew before.

Clue number four: Okay, the number in the units place plus the number in the thousands place = 8, so the number in the units place is 1.

Clue number five: This helps me know that there is one odd number.

Clue number six: The number is 2.

Putting all of the clues together I know that this number is 7,921.

The two numbers are 6,452 and 7,921, and if they never run away again King Googol will have to find someone else to find them!

## Mother Knows Best

1. **(W)**ORK
2. MANSI**(O)**N
3. SH**(R)**INE
4. **(K)**IMONOS
5. SLE**(E)**P
6. WE**(D)**
7. **(B)**ROCADE
8. RIC**(E)**
9. **(T)**EAHOUSE
10. CORMORAN**(T)**
11. M**(E)**RCHANT
12. **(R)**OOMS

Her plan **worked better** than Taro's.